OBD: Obsessive Branding Disorder

O B D
Obsessive Branding Disorder

THE BUSINESS OF ILLUSION
AND THE ILLUSION OF BUSINESS

LUCAS CONLEY

PublicAffairs
New York

Published in the United States by PublicAffairs™,
a member of the Perseus Books Group.

PublicAffairs books are available at special discounts for
bulk purchases in the U.S. by corporations, institutions,
and other organizations. For more information, please
contact the Special Markets Department at the Perseus
Books Group, 2300 Chestnut Street, Suite 200,
Philadelphia, PA 19103, call (800) 810-8145, extension
5000, or e-mail special.markets@perseusbooks.com.

Designed by Brent Wilcox

A CIP data record for this book is available
from the Library of Congress.
ISBN: 978-1-58648-468-2
First Edition

10 9 8 7 6 5 4 3 2 1

For my wife, Laura,
who reads me without words

CONTENTS

Loyalty Beyond
Reason

O God! A beast, that wants discourse of reason.
WILLIAM SHAKESPEARE, *Hamlet*

Ninety-four percent of Japanese women in their twenties own a product made by the French luxury brand Louis-Vuitton.[1] Although Louis-Vuitton charges more than 20 percent more for its products in Japan than in France, some 51 million of Japan's 127 million citizens—40 percent of the entire nation—own one of its products. Part of L-V's inflated price tag in Japan is the result of the costs of shipping. But the primary reason is the inflated value of the brand itself—some Japanese women have admitted forgoing motherhood in order to afford Louis-Vuitton goods.[2]

The act of choosing a material item—in this case, a widely copied leather handbag—over parenthood is indicative of how branded goods can eclipse an individual's sense of self. While an extreme example, the Japanese obsession with Louis-Vuitton is emblematic of a global branding disorder that stands to shift human nature radically, perverting our definition of community and shaping our sense of self. Caught in its throes, society appears to have abandoned reason altogether.

"Loyalty beyond reason" is the doctrine at Saatchi & Saatchi, one of the world's largest advertising firms.* Kevin Roberts, perhaps the most widely recognized and powerful personality in advertising today, is Saatchi's outspoken CEO—a figure reviled and revered for his brash opinions, unorthodox strategies, and penchant for theatrics. A former executive at Pepsi, Roberts once gunned down a Coke vending machine at a corporate event. (The stunt was orchestrated with blanks and fireworks.) Invited to speak to various spy agencies by the U.S. Department of Defense in 2005, he advised the government to rebrand the "War on Terror" as the "Fight for a Better World." Nearing his sixtieth birthday, Roberts is branding's Pied Piper—a man who might be considered the most culpable in having led business astray and fueled our obsession with branding.

The underlying doctrine of Roberts's work is his belief in "loyalty beyond reason," the phenomenon whereby customers are so enamored with a brand that they ignore price, convenience, and competitor parity. To reach this ideal

---

*A subsidiary of the holding company Publicis, Saatchi & Saatchi spans some 153 offices in 85 countries.

state, Roberts counsels his clients to court consumers in such a way that the latter abandon their critical thinking skills. Roberts understands consumer behavior as an emotive, rather than rational, response. In his world, "changing the language" is the equivalent of changing a conversation. In other words, the path to the promised land for brands isn't merchandise or ministration, but marketing.

Is it really that simple? Could a war really be rebranded like a beverage or a bag of cat food, its unsavory characteristics repackaged by way of semantics and bravado? Are consumers so gullible that emotional manipulation will overwhelm their innate reason and logic? Science supports Roberts's position. Emotion has been shown to activate the brain 3,000 times faster than regular thought,[3] and studies in consumer behavior indicate that shoppers are willing to pay up to 200 percent more when their decision is based on emotion rather than reason.[4]

In 2008 an estimated $654 billion will be spent on branding—nearly $300 billion of it in the United States alone.[5] Nowhere else in the world is the concept of branding so readily adopted, so easily transferred from industrial practice to social phenomenon. Today anything with a brand name is vulnerable and anything without one is an opportunity. Water, soil, and concrete now come branded. Need a moment to catch your breath? Branded oxygen is easy to find. Tired? Dozens of entrepreneurs, in clinics and hotels and "nap centers," offer their own proprietary brand of sleep. Branding is encroaching on areas of our lives we never before imagined—from hospitals and education to sex, psychiatry, and cemeteries; we're branded, quite literally, from the cradle to the grave.

Writing for *Fast Company*, a national business magazine centered on themes like innovation, leadership, and technology, has offered me a unique perspective on the trends and obsessions that crisscross the business landscape. Sometimes I don't even have to leave the office to get a good look at them. Each day advance copies of virtually every new business book published in the Western Hemisphere makes its way to our offices. With title after title, in industry after industry, branding books are multiplying. They arrive in FedEx packages from thousands of miles away and in envelopes delivered by bike messenger from offices just up the street. They arrive in bubble wrap, Styrofoam peanuts, and padded yellow sleeves leaking recycled newsprint. Occasionally they arrive naked, gingerly cradled in the hands of their author.

Spilling across my desk, these books offer a cross-section of the credos of capitalism. It's not a pretty picture. Since the industrial age, we've seen countless business theories and management systems, from Taylorism to Trumpegogy, to reengineering and Six Sigma, to lean management, to total quality, to Theory Z. All told, business has accommodated and survived thousands of philosophies, concocted on shop floors and in the halls of academia, discovered in unlikely places like beehives and fish markets. The most popular theories have sparked careers, rocketed books from shelves, and launched entire corporate reorganizations. But eventually each business water-cooler philosophy reached its boiling point and vanished like so much hot air.

More than marketing, advertising, or positioning, branding is an all-in-one ideology—a facile reduction malleable enough to govern all facets of modern business. In the name of the brand, any idea can be defended as valid and any crackpot can assume the status of a guru. And when the snake oil salesmen roll into town shilling branding tonics and salves, anxious executives line up, their minions and dependents standing dutifully at attention. Branding now encompasses supply chains, partnerships, and, in an especially unholy pairing, human resources. Corporate branding books dictate everything from language to dress to the fonts on internal memos. Along the way, the axis has tipped; something has gone awry. Once rooted in the physical world of consumer products, branding has transcended its humble beginnings. Now brands must have a smell, a taste, and a sound. Voices, attitudes, and "processes" must be branded. What was once made up of products and services is now increasingly built out of nebulous intangibles. What was once a brand is now a Brand.

Branding offers a unique example of a business philosophy that has jumped the tracks, barreling through popular culture unchecked. Unlike most business theory, which has traditionally been contained to the business world, with only some specific applications outside of it, the tenets of branding have been embraced by mainstream society. In addition to companies, employees, and products, branding has infected the media we rely on for some degree of objectivity.

Like a pesticide working its way up the food chain, branding reaches the American consumer at many entry points and in heady doses. We're contaminated by the products we buy, the offices in which we work, the advertisements around us, and the news and entertainment we absorb. Our means of communication—from phone to email to instant messaging—are branded, as is our transportation, be it bike, car, train, plane, or boat. Even the people around us—celebrities, financial consultants, and newborns alike—are increasingly branded.

Somewhere between the grocery aisle and gross absurdity, branding has become an epidemic—a mirage turned miracle cure. In the global community in which new media and increasingly fickle stockholders demand immediate results, today's corporations have taken comfort in branding's soothing, vague idealism. A new business religion, branding has risen during an age of confusion; companies have never had less control of their images. Businesses are terrified. Their products are rapidly copied and commodified, rendering innovation obsolete in a matter of days or weeks. The media they rely on for promotion and positioning are splintering and frustrating any attempt to deliver the brand message to consumers in one piece. Investors, demanding fractions of pennies on a quarterly basis, are often storming the gates, ousting executives after just months on the job. Worldwide, annual turnover of CEOs soared 59 percent between 1995 and 2006.[6] CMOs, those executives in charge of branding, now average just 26.8 months on the job.[7] Frazzled and panicked, executives are turning to a niche business strategy formerly reserved for laundry detergents and diapers—one elastic enough to bend outside the reach of reason, but sturdy enough to support its own organized religion (high priests and hucksters included).

When a company's name is stigmatized, a brand can be changed in a flash, even if the business practices behind the colorful new logo and spokesperson remain the same. After all, what is a brand? Nothing we can measure or explain precisely. It's a fictional property, often illusory and evocative—the emperor's finest duds. CEOs swagger through the business pages, dangerously out of touch with reality as they boast about their "brand equity" (the imagined value of a nebulous entity). Hypocrisy prevails. Ford spends billions a year proclaiming that the company is "Driving American Innovation," but its cars average fewer miles per gallon than the old Model T of 1908.* Oil giant BP projects itself as an environmental activist, but oil spills up and down the West Coast, infrastructure negligence, and the country's worst industrial accident in a decade draw a different picture.**

---

*According to the Environmental Protection Agency, Ford's 2007 fleet averaged 18.7 miles per gallon. The 1908 Model T averaged as much as 25 miles per gallon.

**In March 2005, an explosion at a BP refinery in Texas killed 15 workers and injured 170. Regulators ultimately determined that the deaths were "completely preventable."

The effort to distort meaning with words parallels the desire to bypass reason with emotion. It's a fierce and fearsome combo. Reaching beyond reason, branding throws off business's true north. Disoriented, obsessed with surface and sentiment over substance, companies apply their ingenuity to the disingenuous, perfecting names and nuances instead of responding to consumer needs.

Increasingly desperate to control and manage the brand, companies proselytize in wilder and more subversive ways, spending on brand placement wherever they can. Urinals, golf holes, beach sand—no space is off limits for promoting the brand. Even personal conversations aren't taboo: word-of-mouth marketing, wherein companies reward "customer evangelists" for covertly promoting products to their friends and family, is a growth industry. So too are guerrilla, viral, experiential, and sensory marketing.

For a philosophy based on quick fixes and illusion, branding has gone further than anyone imagined. Companies once turned to advertising and marketing firms to spread the word about a new product or service. But over the past fifteen to twenty years, even some of the most established advertising firms have begun calling themselves "brand specialists." Whereas advertisers and marketers tend to reach *out* to broadcast a message, branders often begin by reaching in—attempting to realign the business and resculpt the corporate psyche. By virtue of their access and influence, branders wind up assuming far greater roles than the advertisers and marketers who preceded them. Where an advertising firm might attempt to understand a company's mission and communicate those ideas to consumers in a palatable way, the modern branding firm will often turn the process on its head, reworking the fundamental ideas and values upon which a company has operated for years with an eye toward giving consumers what they may want to hear that moment. Branding has gradually superseded the advertising industry, either claiming advertising outright or dictating the messages that advertisers are allowed to deliver. Increasingly, marketing has also become a division of branding.

Where once a product came with a brand name, today brands are "built" to supersede their products. The most well-known brands—the Apples, the Googles, the Starbucks—are praised for being "greater than the sum of their parts." It's a rosy vision, but a dangerous region in which to root an ideology. Many executives are so focused on the strength of the all-encompassing idea—the Brand—that they ignore the physical properties that compose it.

"The only thing you need to make a profit is a brand," advises Al Reis, consultant, columnist, and author of twelve books on positioning, marketing, and branding— and the branding industry's longest champion. "These days, kids don't dream of growing up to be a rock star or a sports hero," says *Forbes*, the stalwart, ninety-year-old business magazine. "They dream of becoming a leveraged brand."

By abandoning the trusty, dusty principles of business—innovative products, good service, solid management—for the idealism of branding, companies reveal the true escapist appeal of their new religion. Busying themselves with brand ideation meetings, funneling time and money into propping up a shifting, nebulous entity, executives have an alternative to tired old sermons like research and development, customer service, and core competencies. In their place, companies have become fixated on perfecting the tenor of the voice on their on-hold recordings or engineering the smell permeating the box of their latest MP3 player. Millions of dollars are spent aligning the identity and emotional appeal of the brand aura. To those caught in the midst of it all, their frenzied efforts almost feel like genuine work.

Branding is more distraction than progress. Real change results from innovation that advances knowledge and improves the quality of our lives. It's difficult work for deferred and indefinite rewards. In 2006 Ford was the United States' second largest spender on research and development.[8] It also lost $16 billion. Meanwhile, Apple, a leader in design and technical innovation, spends less of its revenue on R&D than the industry average and its profits have soared. It's a gamble.

Branding is quick, persuasive, and relatively cheap. It's about image, impression, and positioning. Branding offers the satisfaction of a sense of change without the hard work. Executives feel good because, technically, it's still innovation—surface innovation. Meanwhile, image is easier and less expensive to work with than products or services. It's an inside-out philosophy devoted to sculpting a subjective and imaginary property. Branding is an ends bottled as a means—sort of like playing a game in reverse. Naturally, executives love the idea of playing when they think they already know the score. They seem to forget that the other team—be it their customers, the media, or rival companies—is not always interested in playing along.

The irony of branding is that its impact is often the opposite of its intent. Branding distracts companies and executives from what they ought to be doing. Though companies pay consultants millions to help develop branded mission statements, 77 percent of U.S. employees don't feel that those statements reflect the way their company does business.[9] Inundated by junk, consumers simply stop listening. Of the five thousand ads the average consumer sees each day, just 1 to 3 percent are remembered without prompting.[10] Even the practitioners of branding are disenchanted with the business of illusion. Only 16 percent of marketers believe that brands make life more meaningful.[11] Yet the obsession with branding continues unabated. Executives crank it out, and repelled consumers counteract the spin by ignoring it. Driving against each other, these forces are creating a whirlwind of self-defeating corporate and consumer behavior.

Early on, the branding phenomenon was limited to a few experts and their hopeful clients. But as the momentum has escalated, more and more of us are being sucked into the vortex. Branded smells, branded towns, people branding themselves—what was humorous to us as a spectator sport is proving horrendous as something we must take part in. All the while, distracted by attempts to find our bearings, we've all but forgotten the billions of dollars being funneled into the branding cyclone, never to emerge again.

Chasing brand equity, U.S. companies obsess over their brand to the point of distraction. Foreign competitors in places like India and China are happy to pick up the slack. Shipping jobs, factories, and entire industries overseas, executives maintain control over what they've convinced themselves is their most valuable equity.

To understand the conditions of business and the vacuum of leadership that have created the environment in which this disorder thrives, I stepped away from the slush pile and the steady stream of branding books parading across my desk and set out to draw back the curtain on a booming industry we encounter everywhere but know little about. What I discovered is a society increasingly warped by an obsessive disorder.

A Branding Company

Town

The city of man serves not only the needs of the body and the demands of commerce but the desire for beauty and the hunger for community. It is a place where men are more concerned with the quality of their goals than the quantity of their goods.

LYNDON BAINES JOHNSON,
"The Great Society," commencement
address, University of Michigan,
Ann Arbor, May 22, 1964

The first time Russell Singletary returned home to New Orleans was three months after the storm, for Thanksgiving 2005. National Guardsmen were still patrolling the streets, and his aunt was living off a closet full of military-issue MREs (meal, ready-to-eat). A native of Algiers, the neighborhood opposite the French Quarter across the Mississippi River, Singletary has only returned once since then.

"People were drinking a lot more than before," he recalls. "Most things were destroyed and just never opened back up. But business at a handful of local shops and restaurants was picking up."

As business picked up, so did the crime rate. On a sunny afternoon in late December 2006, Singletary and a friend were eating lunch in a crowded restaurant in his old neighborhood when two young men, one brandishing a shotgun, entered. Their faces covered with bandanas, they ordered the patrons to the floor and swept through the restaurant, tipping chairs and snapping up wallets and handfuls of cash. Within moments, they had escaped out the back door.

Though everyone in the restaurant was rattled, no one was hurt. In their rush to get away, the thieves had even overlooked Singletary's money. He admits he was lucky; others haven't been as fortunate. Since August 2005, three of Singletary's friends and neighbors have been shot and killed in the streets of New Orleans. The number is much higher, he says, if he includes all the names and faces he has recognized in the obituaries.

Plagued by corruption and deep-seated racial tensions, New Orleans has always wrestled with crime. Violence has been a part of the city's identity for as long as anyone can remember. But in the wake of Hurricane Katrina, the rate of violent crimes like rape, robbery, and assault soared. The city saw 161 murders in 2006, an estimated 69 percent increase over 2004 and the highest percentage per capita of any first-world city that year. The murder rate climbed a further 30 percent in 2007 to 209.[1]

On August 9, 2007, with the city's murder rate on track to top 2006, a local television reporter confronted mayor Ray Nagin about the impact of the city's murders on its tourism business. "It's not good for us," Nagin responded. "But it also keeps the New Orleans brand out there, and it keeps people thinking about our needs and what we need to bring this community back. So it is kind of a two-edged sword." The comment quickly spread throughout the Internet and the national media, inciting outrage and acrimony.

While no one could argue that Nagin stuck his foot in his mouth, the eruption of indignation following his comment about the city's brand sounded suspiciously bombastic. After all, in the years since Katrina, violent crime in New Orleans has become a fact of life—locals live with it on a daily basis; evacuees watch and wait from a distance, biding their time until it's safe to return; the national press has dubbed the city "America's Murder Capital." Yet amid all the histrionics and finger wagging, what really seemed to bother many people wasn't Nagin's insensitivity to murder victims—it was how he had defined the city's brand.

The controversy raised some profound questions about the nature of branding. What is a brand? Is it a reflection of reality? An idealized fiction? Perhaps a little bit of both? Can a place really be branded? And if so, how is it done and who gets the final word?

The press generated by Nagin's comment made one thing abundantly clear—when it comes to New Orleans' brand, residents want to hear "Mardi Gras," not "Murder Capital." It doesn't matter what the FBI says about the murder rate in New Orleans. It doesn't matter that a national poll ranked New Orleans last in terms of safety and cleanliness among major U.S. travel destinations. New Orleans locals expect the same things everyone expects from brands today: a little bit of fallacy sweetened with a whole lot of fantasy.

As it turned out, Nagin's timing couldn't have been worse. City officials had recently launched "Forever New Orleans," an aggressive international branding campaign that included print and online ads, billboards, television commercials, and a thirty-minute prime-time travel show. According to campaign organizers, the multimillion-dollar campaign, funded by U.S. taxpayers, was designed specifically to "overcome misperceptions" about New Orleans with snappy taglines designed to dispel lingering concerns about the conditions in New Orleans after Katrina, like "Soul Is Waterproof" and "New Orleans Is Open. To Just About Anything." By being candid instead of contrived, Nagin was undercutting the city's desperate efforts to rebrand the city and drive tourism by relying on innuendo and clichés.

"It's all about buying beads, ordering a hurricane cocktail, and taking home a poster of a man playing a trumpet under a streetlight," Singletary says. In a post-Katrina New Orleans suffering staggering crime rates and struggling to rebuild, such tired clichés frustrate and disgust many native residents. The storm and its aftermath have become an undeniable part of the city's inherent identity. "The idea that you could just package it up and sell it misses the reality of what's going on," he says. "You can't brand away a bunch of murders."

Shaming Nagin for lacking guile while public funds and resources are devoted to projecting a disingenuous image of New Orleans is odious. But in recent years the calculated branding of cities, states, and countries in the aftermath of disaster has become commonplace. In particular, the rebranding of New Orleans bears some notable similarities to the rebranding of another American city struck by tragedy—one uniquely placed at the heart of the branding industry itself.

□   □   □

What Los Angeles is to plastic surgery, Cincinnati, Ohio, is to the branding business. An estimated one-third of the Fortune 100 have paid for identity-related work here, from minor touch-ups to complete overhauls.[2] Home of Procter & Gamble, the world's largest advertiser, and headquarters for both Kroger supermarkets, the nation's largest grocery-only supermarket chain, and Macy's Inc., the country's leading department store operator, Cincinnati is an obvio hub for the many A-list branding outfits that now crowd its downtown.

Thousands of professionals live and work in Cincinnati, earning billions of dollars a year branding everything from tubes of toothpaste to entire nations. Beyond the products one expects to be branded and packaged, an unlikely host of products, including charities, public schools, and flower shows, are also absorbed in branding campaigns. The reach of branding and its desirability as a tool to enhance and sell ideas is visible on any Cincinnati street.

Inside LPK (Libby Perszyk Kathman), the largest independent branding firm in the world, branders devote themselves to fine-tuning the look and feel of products in an effort to define their clients' goods in the virtual sea of mass consumption. At 9:00 AM on a summer morning, with cool air pumping through the candy-slick offices, branding strategist John Recker is blazing through a PowerPoint presentation highlighting the branding of Froot Loops cereal. Bright orange, red, and yellow Os flash across the screen in a flurry of cheery cartoon exuberance. A jumbo Technicolor Toucan Sam beams encouragingly from the box on the screen as Recker describes how LPK "develops and supports the atmosphere of Froot Loops."

The LPK headquarters teams with branders striving to "develop and support the atmosphere" of the world around us. A large portion of the products on U.S. grocery store shelves (the number of which has more than tripled since 1991[3]) is branded here. Each floor of LPK's eight-story headquarters is dedicated to a particular product medium—beauty products, food, technology. Looking around at ninety-six thousand feet of branding obsession, I can easily imagine that Willy Wonka's factory had set about designing fancy wrappers rather than candy.

According to Jerry Kathman, LPK's president and CEO, roughly five thousand people around the world create the look of 90 percent of what Americans buy. Four hundred of those individuals work for him. Whether or not Kathman is exaggerating is difficult to know. Founded in 1919, LPK has recently done "image work" for IBM, Samsung, Microsoft, and AT&T, to name a few. But even a star-studded portfolio isn't as impressive as it sounds in an industry of cyclonic change. Clients that can afford to do so molt their logos, mottos, and mission statements regularly, typically shedding their branding firm in the process. Supporting and developing the atmosphere of AT&T, for example, has had its ups and downs. The year 2006 marked AT&T's twenty-third branding campaign in twenty-five years. The cost of the 2006 campaign ("Your World. Delivered.") was an estimated $800 million to $1 billion.[4] Meanwhile, within the maelstrom of brand shifts, customers have been trying to sort out whether they're supposed to pay AT&T Corp, Bell South, SBC Communications, Cingular, or AT&T Inc.

Formerly the executive vice president and director of brand strategy and operations, Recker is Kathman's number two. The title on his business card now reads Chief Strategy Officer. A commanding presence with prematurely gray hair, Recker looks like he'd be equally at home shouting orders to a battalion of armed men in a bunker.

As I listen to Recker describe the creation of a brand identity, it's clear that from his point of view, branding is more than a logo and a tagline. But each new slide presented only seems to illustrate the arbitrary and disingenuous nature of the branding process. Sensing my confusion, Recker explains that branding is "about the organization of tangible elements that results in a manifestation of a considered plan." Allowing little time for this to sink in, he moves on to "embedded value triggers" and the Froot Loops "Tool Box Vision," LPK lingo for the central icons and ideas used to support and develop a brand.

Branding a children's cereal is seemingly quite complex. "Developing and supporting the atmosphere" of Froot Loops involves countless hours of market research, creative brainstorming, design execution, and close collaboration between Kellogg's executives and the branders at LPK. The result is the Tool Box Vision, a blueprint for realizing the Froot Loops brand that outlines all of its elements, from which colors and fonts may be used on products (including fruit chews, cereal bars, and waffles) to the brand's envisioned identity in the market. While it's debatable whether or not so much thought and energy ought to be spent on the presentation of a children's cereal, the concept behind branding isn't difficult to grasp: it all boils down to sales. If Kellogg's executives understand that consumers respond better to a clean, consistent, and clearly positioned product effected by unified fonts and colors, they'll make the necessary changes.

For all LPK's terms and formulas, however, and in spite of Recker's strident delivery and confidence, the more he describes branding, the more it appears to consist entirely of vague idealism and seemingly vain efforts to create something meaningful and permanent from what is often superfluous and transient. The simpler the product, the more byzantine the branding seems.

True to its branded roots, Cincinnati is undergoing re-branding treatments of its own, as are several of its prominent branding firms. As new techniques in consumer persuasion and image creation are imagined, vetted, and popularized, the city offers a glimpse of where we're headed, as well as a penetrating example of a national disorder.

"We need to romance the experience of anything we deal with," Recker says with zeal, by way of further explaining branding at LPK. With this, he flips to a slide of an IBM scanner. The label on the box reads, "Color Flatbed Scanner." From the look of disinterest on Recker's face, I can tell something is wrong. Indeed, when the projector stutters, a bright new box appears, emblazoned with the word "Ideascan." This is the "after" slide of the product once it's been through a solid round of LPK branding. Before I can ask whether consumers will know what "Ideascan" means, Recker is marching onward, flipping through before-and-after shots of one "romanced" product after the next. IBM's "2-Button Mouse" is reborn as "Scrollpoint," and "124-key Keyboard" inexplicably transforms into "RapidAccess."

□   □   □

Procter & Gamble, the number-one maker of household products on earth, is the reason Cincinnati is referred to as the fertile crescent of branding. By the most recent count, 23 of Procter & Gamble's more than 250 brands earn revenues of $1 billion a year or more.[5] Referred to affectionately around town as "billion-dollar brands," they are the jewels in the Queen City's crown.

Of the 140,000 people working for Procter & Gamble in 80 countries around the world, more than 12,000 of them are based in and around the renowned "Dolly Parton Towers," the twin-domed headquarters of Procter & Gamble. Suckling at the teat of the $76 billion branding cash cow are more than 1,000 branding consultants—from designers and ethnographers to linguists and neuroscientists.

Quaint shops and restaurants line Vine Street, one of the city's main commercial areas just outside LPK's offices. Locals line up for the "Five-Way" at Skyline Chili, a regional favorite comprising a heaping portion of beans, onions, and ground beef over a bowl of spaghetti and piled high with shredded cheddar cheese. In JeanRo Bistro, office workers, their ties tucked in their shirts or thrown over their shoulders, huddle over steaming cups of fragrant French onion soup, the house specialty. The newly reopened Fountain Square is dotted with a friendly crowd of business-casual lunchers. It is a definitively Midwest picture: middle-class, middle managers, mostly white.

Just one hundred yards to the east are signs of another city. A dingy parallel to Vine, Race Street also runs through the heart of Cincinnati, albeit with far less foot traffic. Hair salons and the odd Cajun restaurant stick out amid the shuttered storefronts. Young black men in idle groups of twos and threes loiter in newspapered doorways. Vagrants panhandle on corners. There is an aura of purgatory to Race Street; the atmosphere of poverty is made only more poignant by the chipper pace of commerce one block away. The two parallel streets are a reminder of the contrasts and complexities found in any major city.

□   □   □

In the late afternoon of April 9, 2001, the American flag flying outside Cincinnati's District 1 police headquarters was hoisted into the air upside down. Gathered below, an angry crowd of nearly one thousand protesters was demanding answers the police couldn't offer. Why had Timothy Thomas been killed? A brick sailed through the doors of the station. It wasn't long before smoking cans of tear gas were issued back and rioting began.

The 2001 Cincinnati riots led news around the country, burning images into the public eye of rioters pushing shopping carts full of TVs, liquor, and furniture and police marching shoulder to shoulder past burning Dumpsters on eerily empty streets. Americans hadn't seen riots of a similar scale since the 1992 acquittal of four L.A. police officers in the beating of Rodney King.

Race relations in Cincinnati are decades behind much of the rest of the country. In 1994 the Ku Klux Klan marched through the center of town and erected a cross in Fountain Square. Crucifix burnings and race-related hate crimes make headlines in the area every year. Fifteen minutes north of the city, just off the interstate, a barn roof has been painted with a massive Confederate flag.

Cincinnati and its police department were already embroiled in a federal class-action lawsuit with the American Civil Liberties Union over allegations of racial profiling when Timothy Thomas was killed. Nineteen years old, black, and unarmed, Thomas was shot in the heart by a white police officer as he ran through a dark alley in a drug-infested neighborhood. He was the fifteenth black male under age forty to die at the hands of Cincinnati police since 1995. The numbers didn't look good. No white men had been killed during the same six-year period, and Thomas's was the fourth such death in the city in just six months.

For three days in 2001 the city raged. Residents of leafy suburbs like Milton and Wyoming rose from their beds to images of city hall under siege. Rioters in the downtown metropolitan area were burning storefronts, assaulting police, and pulling white drivers from their cars and beating them in the street.

Fires lit up the city. One police officer was shot, and another was burned by a rioter's Molotov cocktail. On the third day of rioting, mayor Charles Luken declared a state of emergency. Citizens were instructed to "stay in their homes and pray." The following day, as the president of the NAACP arrived in town, the riots subsided.

Emerging from their homes, residents took stock. In the following months, some set about healing race relations in the community. Others worked to establish new rules to ensure that police were properly trained. And some began to discuss what could be done about Cincinnati's tarnished image.

□   □   □

For a community of image experts, the wave of national disgust and horror after the Cincinnati riots was difficult to bear. "With our branding expertise, it's no wonder people were walking around with their heads hanging low," recalls Phil Duncan, a branding specialist with Landor Associates, a global branding firm with offices in Cincinnati and one of the city's premier firms. The estimated damage of the civil unrest in Cincinnati topped $14 million.[6] Beyond the financial toll, the riots generated a lot of bad press, a particularly poignant blow to such an image-conscious community.

For months the city struggled to come to terms with what had happened. When the debate over how to mend race relations finally quieted, questions began surfacing about how to fix Cincinnati's image. "A city that preferred to keep its racial problems quiet was now the talk of the nation," declared the *Cincinnati Enquirer*. "A city that prided itself on law and order was now a symbol of chaos."[7] In light of the fact that the riots were always in the headlines, some in Cincinnati saw the *Enquirer* as part of the problem.

"God love the *Enquirer*," Phil Duncan chuckles, "but it's not exactly tourism-friendly." An authority on image creation and control, Duncan understands the importance of a reputation. As one of the branding chieftains at Landor Associates, he watched Cincinnati take a beating in the media. Duncan feared that the riots would scar Cincinnati for years. So did Ellen van der Horst, future president of the Cincinnati Chamber of Commerce, and Scott Usitalo, soon to be the head of the CincinnatiUSA Regional Tourism Network. All experienced branders, each was deeply affected by the riots and worried about their lasting effect on Cincinnati's image.

Van der Horst was at a conference in Philadelphia when she got word that rioting had begun. Right away the city's image was on her mind. "My personal reaction was one of huge disappointment and concern about how it would be perceived and how the story would be told," she says.

"Our image was being filled by the news," says Scott Usitalo. "Not the image we wanted to get out." He knew something had to be done to protect the city's reputation. "From a traveler's perspective, you go to the Web to find what the city has to offer," says Usitalo. "Cincinnati.com is owned by the newspapers, so if you want to know what is going on in Cincinnati, what you get is the headlines. That family of four would find headlines about that civil unrest and say, 'Oh, my. We don't want to go there!'"

Duncan, Usitalo, and van der Horst all began at P&G, managing big brands. After the riots they found themselves in a position to brand the city by way of an ambitious multimillion-dollar campaign.

While it may seem presumptuous for a handful of former branders to reshape the identity of an entire city, it's difficult to overplay the power and reach of Proctor & Gamble, the company where they earned their stripes. Founded in 1837, P&G is legendary for turning bars of soap and potato chips into iconic brands—friends of the family. The biggest advertiser in the nation, Procter & Gamble's advertising budget was $4.9 billion in 2006—the largest in the world.[8] According to Procter & Gamble, its hundreds of brands "touch the lives" of consumers 3 billion times a day.

As the area's largest employer and the world's foremost authority on supporting and developing the atmosphere of household products, Procter & Gamble would inevitably have had a stake in the city's image overhaul. After the riots, tourism was down, the city center was empty after 5:00 PM, and convincing professionals to relocate their families to a shrinking Midwest city like Cincinnati was much harder than it had been. A subsequent boycott of downtown Cincinnati businesses, led by influential African American celebrities like Bill Cosby, Whoopi Goldberg, Wynton Marsalis, and Smokey Robinson, is estimated to have cost the city more than $10 million in tourism and entertainment revenues.[9] Something had to be done to turn the city around. In a brand-centric community, a new brand seemed like the answer. After all, as Duncan would later declare, "in many ways, Cincinnati is just another product on life's shelf."

□   □   □

Place branding, or destination branding, is a fast-growing segment of the branding industry. Branding initiatives are alive and well in places as disparate as Sarasota, Florida, Wagnanui, New Zealand, and almost every country in Africa. (Though the average life span in Africa is shorter now than it was thirty years ago, millions of dollars are being spent glazing over the continent's image.) Consistently ranked among the top three most corrupt nations in the world, Nigeria launched the $3 million Nigerian Image Project in 2004. The branding campaign has since been relaunched as the Heart of Africa Project. After its thirty-four-day war with Hezbollah in Lebanon, Israel ranked last in the 2006 Nation Brand Index (NBI), a study of thirty-six countries' brands. BIG, the Brand Israel Group, now aims to reposition the country with a strategy of "downplaying religion and avoiding any discussion of the conflict with the Palestinians."[10] Said the *Jewish Week*, "Think of Israel as a product undergoing an overhaul to make it more competitive in the marketplace. What's called for are fewer stories explaining the rationale for the security fence, and more attention to scientists doing stem-cell research on the cutting edge."[11]

When it comes to manipulating image in the name of place brands, the United States is in a league of its own. Like a state bird or flower, every state *requires* a brand. The State Brand Index, an "analytical ranking of the brands of all U.S. States," can be purchased for $32,000. Half of the convention and visitors' bureaus in the country have opened their wallets to branding's snake oil salesmen. The results are worthy of a Woody Allen satire. Most "place brands" are vague, interchangeable, and ultimately forgettable, such as "As Big as You Think" (Kansas—$1.7 million per year), "We Love Dreamers" (Oregon—$2 million per year), and "Possibilities . . . Endless" (Nebraska—the twelfth state slogan since 1972).[12]

Despite the most earnest efforts, place branding often goes over like a lead balloon. In 1999, at the height of the dot-com boom, Seattle was rebranded as See@L. Residents eventually tired of the cutism, and sixteen months and $200,000 later, they had a new brand: Metronatural. Washington State paid a thirty-two-member "brand development task force" $442,000 over eighteen months to develop and promote "SayWA." Branders intended for the slogan, and its subsequent marketing campaign, to capture and distill a sense of wonder about the state and all it has to offer. Unimpressed, local and national press roundly mocked the idea, killing the campaign just six months after its launch.[13]

After spending some $200,000 on branding research, residents of Pittsburgh and southwest Pennsylvania scoffed at the area's prescribed forty-five-word "brand essence,"* sixteen-word "brand promise," and twelve-word "core theme."[14] It's easy to understand residents' frustration when the branding campaign came at a cost of $2,740 a word for fairly run-of-the-mill copy.

Similar place-branding stories of waste and folly are being repeated around the country. New Jersey dumped

---

*Brand essence: "Just as the steel from which it draws its roots, Pittsburgh has an authenticity and durability that provides a strong foundation, yielding new opportunities to grow and succeed. The amalgamation of our resources draws people together to a place where ideas are invented and transformed." Brand promise: "We will connect you to the people, resources, and communities you need to accomplish your goals." Core theme: "Accomplishment through connected individuality—linking vital individuals, vital communities, and vital resources."

one recent $260,000 rebranding effort, "New Jersey: We'll Win You Over," a day before launch.[15] Branders scooped up a reported $76,000 for suggesting that the city of Galveston, Texas, change its name to "the City of Galveston Island" and embrace "Talk Like a Pirate Day." Citizens didn't warm to either recommendation.[16] Kentucky paid $2.85 million and handed out another $18 million in ad dollars for Kentucky's "Unbridled Spirit" brand. The firm that developed the brand, Louisville-based New West, was paid for everything from creating the slogan and logo to writing speeches, media placement, event planning—and even for some things it apparently never did. (Following an audit of the branding campaign, the state's attorney general, Greg Stumbo, announced that taxpayers had been overbilled by nearly $1.4 million.)[17]

Considering how costly and often vague and impotent place brands can be, the lengths to which branders go to enforce them are comical. The fastidious rules given to employees of Eastern Kentucky University to help maintain the integrity of Kentucky's "Unbridled Spirit" campaign offer strict guidelines to protect the brand's integrity. (Among other restrictions, the Kentucky logo can only be displayed on a solid background, it cannot be crowded out by other logos, and the colors and fonts with which the brand can be displayed are limited.) Branders in Connecticut assigned a "State Curve," dictating specific instructions for how the state's logo ought to be printed. Dividing the state into five regions, branders assigned each one a "color": spring (Litchfield Hills), sunrise (Greater New Haven), plum (Fairfield County), charisma (River Valley), and aqua (Mystic Country). "The psychology of color was used to further define the brand by zeroing on geographic characteristics or more ethereal elements," explained Edward Dombroskas, a Connecticut tourism director, upon the launch of the campaign in 2005. "The result is a branding program built on an incredible amount of research and strategic and creative thinking."[18]

□   □   □

Kentucky and Connecticut are just a couple of examples of the many branding initiatives that illustrate the pervasiveness of a particularly American disorder. Today it goes without saying that, just like product, place must be formalized in terms of a brand—often by way of a costly consulting process. When it came time to launch Cincinnati's rebranding, the experts were all homegrown. This turned out to be a fortunate turn of events, as the rebranding of Cincinnati was more involved than most citywide branding projects.

Unlike the majority of major U.S. cities, Cincinnati is not a one-state city. Perched on the Ohio River along the southern border of the state of Ohio, Cincinnati's metropolitan area spans fifteen counties in three different states—Ohio, Kentucky, and Indiana (each of which, naturally, has its own state brand). To rebrand the city the collaboration of three counties was necessary to adopt a unified look and feel and to pool local money to subsidize the overall marketing of the metropolitan Cincinnati brand. The key, as Duncan put it, was getting the smaller towns and counties to "put aside their little 'burb needs and wear a regional hat that puts money in everyone's pocket." Spearheading the Cincinnati branding effort was Charlotte Otto, a longtime employee of Procter & Gamble; as a vice president, she is the company's global external relations officer and its first female corporate executive.

Though her days of managing brands ended in 1989, Otto saw an opportunity after the riots and quickly recruited Proctor & Gamble's client director to assist with the project. "Charlotte was the ringmaster," recalls Duncan. "She said, 'This would be a fabulous opportunity to define things. I think we can really do this well, and we'd all benefit. Phil, are you in?'" Duncan laughs. "You can't look at Charlotte and say no. You get sucked in." And why not? Having earned his stripes at Procter & Gamble brands like Crest, Tide, and Secret, Duncan had roots there—and Landor, with more experience branding places than most branding shops, was a natural for the project. Just a few years before, Hong Kong had hired the firm to define its brand. Madrid and Pittsburgh both came to Landor, as did West Virginia and Ohio. Landor had rebranded the entire country of Jordan; Cincinnati would be a breeze. As the managing director of Proctor &

Gamble's Cincinnati and Chicago offices, Duncan volunteered Landor's help for free. Scott Usitalo was brought in soon afterward. A Procter & Gamble employee for twenty-five years, Usitalo worked as a brand manager with Pringles, Folgers, Crisco, Duncan Hines, and Vidal Sassoon. When he elected to retire early, Otto approached him with a list of projects to tackle in his final year with the company. He elected to work with Otto and Duncan to develop the regional brand. As an "executive on loan" to the branding effort, Usitalo's experience as a brand manager gave him the right credentials.

Usitalo headed up the CincinnatiUSA Regional Tourism Network, an agency devoted to marketing Cincinnati in nearby cities like Columbus and Louisville (a job he left in 2007). The work included promoting tourism, luring new business to the area, and championing local events, such as the annual "World's Largest Chicken Dance and Hokey Pokey." "What our company does now is take the CinUSA brand and celebrate it to overcome the civil unrest in 2001," said Usitalo. "Overcoming that negative image was the objective."

□   □   □

Cincinnati isn't the first city to receive the Froot Loops treatment; Queen's City branding professionals have been taking their expertise home with them to the suburbs for years. But the manner in which they brand their communities—that is, the image and atmosphere they work to "support and develop" at home—bears a noticeable difference from the branding they perform for the products, companies, and communities they sell.

This irony is particularly pronounced in the sleepy town of Wyoming, Ohio. Six miles north of Cincinnati and the twin-domed towers, Wyoming is a picture of small-town harmony. Life is good in this 125-year-old suburb, home to some eight thousand affluent and middle-class residents. The local school system ranks in the top ten nationally, more than a dozen public parks span the tiny community of less than three square miles, and the town recycles more of its waste than any other in the county.

The residents of Wyoming have good reason to be proud of their town. In recent years, Wyoming, named one of the "prettiest painted places in America," has been honored as a "Tree City USA," and it landed a spot on the National Register of Historic Places. This is not your average Midwest burb—and the residents of Wyoming intend to keep it that way. They've even got a ten-year master plan.

Developed by the town's own Master Plan Committee, Wyoming's ten-year plan describes the community as "the modern village." The plan is, in essence, Wyoming's own "Tool Box Vision"—an outline of the fundamental ideas and principles the town intends to use to guide its brand in the years ahead. In 1997, when the plan was established, the committee envisioned such goals as "a village pace and a comfortable size. [Wyoming] is a place where we know and greet our neighbors, where we can walk to school and shopping. People are friendly and work at maintaining social networks within the community. Public recreational facilities are abundant and accessible. We have a sense of pride about our town."

The residents of Wyoming like their home just the way it is, thank you. Carefully considered community guidelines preserve the small-town look and feel. Strict zoning laws protect local small businesses, keeping big businesses and chain stores at bay.

There's a certain duplicity—and a certain appropriateness—to the protective stance toward their community that Wyoming's branding residents have taken. After all, the town is home to a number of Cincinnati's designers and brand managers, the very men and women who spend their days dreaming up the attention-grabbing advertisements, experiential marketing programs, and general branding bonanza the rest of the country puts up with every day.

"Wyoming is about the calculated management of no messages," says Wyoming resident Don Childs, vice president and chief creative officer at laga, a Cincinnati-based branding outfit. "It's a green, lush community. There's kind of a Mayberry feel to it."

Childs moved to the area from Chicago in 1999. After living in Ohio for eight years, he says the traffic is the worst part about visiting his old home. Commenting on his new stomping grounds—home to retired Procter & Gamble CEO John Pepper for nearly thirty years—he admits that he's thrilled at the strictness of the zoning laws and the lack of franchises. "There's no branding. It's pure."

□   □   □

Following the riots, Cincinnati's rebranding process began with conversations with local residents. Devoting as many as ten employees at a time to the project, Landor oversaw fifteen community sessions, where fifteen to thirty people discussed what Cincinnati meant to them. Between these discussions and online questionnaires, the firm gathered more than five thousand responses. Overall, Cincinnati residents were surprised to learn how much their city actually had to offer. The findings were the inspiration for Cincinnati's new tagline, "All Together Surprising."

The experts dubbed the city brand "CincinnatiUSA," not only to tap American pride but also to reflect, literally, the city's inseparability from the nation. The logo, a tricolor bridge divided in thirds, is symbolic of the three-state region. "We had everything from classic designers to linguists and naming experts working on it. We devoted thousands of man-hours," says Duncan. "We have a brand driver process involving focused brainstorming and ideation. We invested in this program as if it was a big corporate brand that we were about to launch." Had Landor billed the city, Duncan estimates that the two-year process would have cost between $150,000 and $200,000.

While Duncan headed up the development process, Usitalo at the Regional Tourism Network marketed the finished product, using the CincinnatiUSA brand as a theme for packaging local attractions and deals on area hotel rooms. The RTN is guided by a three-member board: one person each from the convention and visitors' bureaus in Kentucky and Cincinnati (both of which contribute to the RTN's $2 million marketing budget with hotel taxes) and an executive from Procter & Gamble. (Anyone who contributes $1 million or more gets a spot on the board.)

Ellen van der Horst joined Folger's right out of college and spent several years with Procter & Gamble before leaving in 1983. Now the president of the Cincinnati Chamber of Commerce, she ensures that the chamber is doing all that it can to reinforce the city's branding initiative. The number of community groups adopting the brand is growing. Besides the Chamber of Commerce and the RTN, Cincinnati's downtown Fountain Square recently updated its logo (yes, the square has its own logo) with colors and design elements from the logo created by Landor. "Other communities are connecting to the brand in their printed materials," she says. "What's emerging is a unified look, feel, and message."

❑　　❑　　❑

Though unifying cities, states, and nations under one logo and tagline may occasionally boost tourism revenues, complexity is what enables a unique approach. Companies are no different. Applying a top-down, outside-in branding process to everything from customer service to human resources is little more than a small-minded effort to lacquer a diverse institution with an easily recallable catchphrase. Ramming the multifaceted personality of a place or company into a simplistic "brand essence" insults the intended audience's intelligence, whether it be the consumer or the employee. Meticulously managing your identity implies that your actions are somehow separate from that identity. A brand is something to be controlled rather than any expression of authenticity.

Rather than devoting the time and money it would take to make Cincinnati a better place, branding specialists have put their energies toward "supporting and developing the atmosphere" of an idealized city—in essence, boxing it up and selling it to outsiders as another product on life's shelf. Instead of spreading the word about all the attractions that Cincinnati has to offer among "all together surprised" locals, the city's branders devoted their funds to projecting an image to outsiders.

"I'm not sure that Joe-on-the-street is even aware of it," says Otto of the city's new packaging. "Indianapolis, Louisville, St. Louis . . . the meaningful bucks are spent outside the region."

The image work done in Cincinnati stands as a model of branding prowess. The city has seen a dramatic increase in crime over the past several years: between 1999 and 2006, Cincinnati rose from the 107th most dangerous U.S. city to the 16th, according to the annual analysis of FBI data.[19] Despite this, the general public has long forgotten the underlying racial tensions and chronic problems with crime brought to light by the 2001 riots. And as with New Orleans, local officials often appear more concerned with protecting the contrived brand than with offering a candid brief. "Don't get caught up in the comparative statistical analysis," claimed police chief Thomas Streicher Jr. of Cincinnati's crime rate in October 2007. "We really don't have an issue with crime."[20]

□   □   □

As innocuous as the phrase sounds, "supporting and developing the atmosphere" of a brand is often about propagating misperceptions, creating "perceived functionality," and covering up shortcomings—whether the effort is on behalf of something as simple as a children's cereal or as complex as a city. American companies are turning to this type of illusory branding in order to keep their products on the shelves of high-volume big-box retailers. The shift is taking its toll: once the most innovative in the world by far, U.S. companies are losing ground fast to less expensive Asian brands and private-label goods.

To compete within the environment of the staggering sales volume and enormous efficiencies of scale offered by big-box retailers like Wal-Mart, U.S. companies are "feeding the monster": cutting back on R&D, operating on razor margins, and meeting faster product cycles. They are banking on illusion, not innovation, to stay alive.

Feeding the
Monster

In large consumer-goods companies . . .
brands are the raison d'être. They are the
focus of decision making and the basis of accountability. They are the fiefdoms, run by the
managers with the biggest jobs and the
biggest budgets. And never have those managers been rewarded for shrinking their turfs.

Harvard Business Review, 2004

I n 2000 Procter & Gamble's CEO, Alan G. Lafley, told his
brand managers and researchers to start looking outside the company for product ideas, setting a 50–50
target for external and internal innovations. Previously,
90 percent of Procter & Gamble's new products and innovative formulas came from its own research and development labs. But between the time Lafley was appointed

CEO in June 2000 and June 2001, the company posted losses of $320 million. Wall Street dumped the stock from just shy of $60 to less than $30. Something had to change. In a daring strategy, Procter & Gamble invited outsiders to peddle their innovations while its brand managers stuck to what they were best at.

Lafley's philosophy of looking outside the company also extended to acquisitions; since 2000, Procter & Gamble has acquired several billion-dollar brands from other companies, including Clairol and Wella. The $57 billion acquisition of Gillette brought in five more—Mach3, Duracell, Right Guard, Braun, and Oral B. Outsourcing at the Procter & Gamble brand giant has also increased. IT was handed over to Hewlett-Packard years ago. The manufacturing of the iconic Ivory brand is now subcontracted to a Canadian firm. Lafley is effectively streamlining Procter & Gamble, leveraging the company's branding expertise and shedding whatever else he can.

By late 2006, the company had reached its goal: 50 percent of its new products and formulas now came from outside the company.[1] In 2007 revenues topped $76 billion, and P&G has continued its rebound, trading above $65 a share in early 2008. Today, when new product ideas come in, Procter & Gamble brand managers can decide where to place them. (They determine, for example, whether the new stain-fighting pen is a good fit for Mr. Clean or Tide.)

Challenged in recent years by overseas companies that can quickly and easily replicate products, long-standing

American manufacturers like Procter & Gamble have been forced to leverage more than their products' conventional features and to rethink how to market products that are virtually indistinguishable through brand equity. Or, in the words of Kevin Roberts, they must now get consumers to commit to loyalty beyond reason.

Just up the street from Procter & Gamble's corporate headquarters in Cincinnati, the United States Playing Card Company (USPCC) exemplifies just how challenged established brands have been in a rapidly shifting marketplace. The famed makers of Aviator, Bee, Bicycle, and Hoyle cards, as well as a number of other games and puzzles (including the infamous "most wanted" deck of cards commissioned by the Defense Department during the 2003 invasion of Iraq), USPCC has been producing cards and games for 140 years. Bicycle, its best-known brand, is the most trusted card in the world: the choice of Vegas casinos and poker tournaments, it is regarded as the gold standard among many magicians and for a century has been the best-selling playing card on the market. But fueled by the recent surge in poker's popularity and the high margins of selling layered paper and polymeric plastic film for several dollars a deck, cheap alternatives and Bicycle knockoffs began to challenge USPCC. Lacking any tricks up its sleeves to further differentiate itself in the market, USPCC had to swallow its pride and call up the branders. But when the product is as simple as a playing card or a poker chip, there's not much that branding can do. Even Bicycle Pro—a new line of cards with a slightly retooled bicycle pattern and easier-to-read symbols—isn't much of a change to the average consumer. Especially when competing decks of cards sell for less than half the cost.

Bicycle's story is common. The rise in quality of private-label brands and knockoffs from Asia is forcing iconic brands to appeal to Cincinnati's branding specialists for a leg up on the competition. Increased pressure from mega-retailers like Wal-Mart and Target is simultaneously pressuring companies to update the look of their products and to launch endless line extensions in an effort to draw consumers' attention.

□   □   □

More than thirty-five thousand new products are released every year.[2] By most estimates, more than nine out of ten will fail by year's end. Inundated with choices, consumers have adapted, even in the face of increasingly shorter product cycles. Who hasn't grown accustomed to a certain product—a specially formulated moisturizer, a certain kind of makeup, or just the right deodorant scent—only to see it discontinued to make room for the new line? Like junkies, we're growing hooked on newer, faster, more specialized, and more limited products. And major retailers are happy to deliver at an accelerating rate. At such a pace, there's hardly any room for significant innovations to reach the market, let alone take hold with consumers.

"We've gotten so into this mass media frenzy, and the big retailers are trying to keep step with that," says laga's Julie Anixter. "There's Wal-Mart over here getting NASCAR M&Ms to you the day after the guy wins the race! It's all about giving consumers what they want at a moment's notice. When Wal-Mart wants new brands, Procter & Gamble listens—it's 'feed the monster.'" So, rather than investigating a better formula for motor oil, why not simply change the shape of the bottle? And instead of actually improving the anti-wrinkle cream, give it a new name.

No surprise, this is exactly what most branding firms are prepared to do. It's either that or turn away the business and go broke. By the looks of the firms in Cincinnati, none are passing up the profits. Take Procter & Gamble's Herbal Essences. Originally designed as a back-to-nature brand for holistic consumers, with branders' help the shampoo evolved into an innuendo-charged, tongue-in-cheek orgasm in a bottle before morphing into a neon package with lots of fruity imagery.

Like the image-oriented services they offer, nearly all of the major branding outfits in Cincinnati boast slick, glossy offices with original design elements and high-end furniture in upscale locales. At Interbrand, most of the walls are metal, covered in heavy-duty magnets or doubling as marker boards. As branders are inspired, they can leave a note midway down the hallway. In 2006 LPK expanded its operations, acquiring a nineteenth-century mansion and neighboring modernist building in downtown Cincinnati.

□   □   □

From his office at LPK's headquarters, Jerry Kathman can see the future. "You're not going to out-feature your competition," the CEO claims. "We're in an image-based culture, and companies have realized they need a lot more rigor as far as their identity is concerned. We're a tiny industry, yet we get into the C-suites [the offices of the chief decision-makers], and we're making an impact far beyond the world of branding and design." His belief, and that of many other branders, is that conditions will only get better for the design industry in the years ahead. Judging by the rate at which branding is outpacing innovation, he's probably right. Rather than try to build a better mousetrap, companies are looking for better ways to brand their existing products. Some, like M&Ms, can afford to "feed the monster" with new packaging and constant product tweaks. Others have to look for more creative solutions.

Many of the iconic Western brands that built up their names during the twentieth century are suddenly finding themselves "victims" of low-cost competitors out of Asia, India, South America, and elsewhere. Established Western brands aren't competing on price alone either; today they're challenged by illegitimate copycats and government-subsidized imports alike.

As Asian brands have expanded their reach into the Western world, they've grown savvy about the power that brand names can offer. Just twenty years ago, China had less than ten industrial design programs. There are over four hundred today, and according to Peter Lawrence, former director of the Design Management Institute and chairman of the Corporate Design Foundation, most of them have sprung up in the past decade. Lawrence notes that China may now be graduating as many as ten thousand designers a year.

Not that all ten thousand are landing jobs in industrial design—only 25 percent do. Despite its roaring economy, China has not especially distinguished itself in the realm of branding. Some Chinese companies, rather than getting lost in the nuances of building a modern brand from scratch, have resorted to buying out well-known Western brands as they expand into Western markets. Lenovo spent $1.75 billion on IBM's PC unit in 2005. BenQ, a Taiwanese "manufacturer of networking lifestyle devices" (cell phones), picked up German company Siemens's cell-phone subsidiary the same year. In December 2006, Techtronic, a Hong Kong–listed power tool company, "steadily building a stable of established and internationally recognized brands with dynamic growth potential," bought the ailing one-hundred-year-old Ohio vacuum brand Hoover for $107 million.

Then there are the shadow brands—inexpensive, familiar offerings with names like Soby (electronics), Chery (cars), and Prado (handbags). Chery Automobile, China's fourth-largest automaker and the country's largest automotive exporter, has been frustrating U.S.-based Chevrolet (a.k.a. Chevy) for years. It's not just the similar name either. In 2005 Chery sold a vehicle called the QQ that was virtually identical to one of Chevrolet's Daewoo models, the Spark. Chevrolet sued, and Chery settled out of court. (Though Chery sells cars in the Middle East, Asia, and South America, a deal to launch the brand in the United States in 2007 fell through.)

Others continue to pop up—each illegitimate copycat something of a legitimizing compliment. Honda had its Hongda, Rover its Roewe, and Wal-Mart its Wumart. The *Wall Street Journal* caught China Unicom openly acknowledging on its website that its Redberry phone was piggybacking on Research in Motion's Blackberry brand. The Redberry name was—according to the company—picked to "extend the image and name of 'BlackBerry' that people are already familiar with."[3]

Beyond slow-moving lawsuits, major brands sometimes retaliate against unfair competition by hiring teams of private investigators and outsourcing the cloak-and-dagger work to super-secret research firms with close relationships to government agencies.

Joe Loomis, founder of one such investigative outfit, Net Enforcers, equates his job with that of a plumber "fixing a leaky pipe." Owing to the sensitive nature of its work, Net Enforcers operates from an undisclosed location.* Loomis's thirty-five-plus employees, the majority of whom have investigative backgrounds, spend their days tracking down counterfeit and "gray market" (illegally distributed bonafide products) for companies like Alpine and JVC. Net Enforcers' employees research, buy, and inspect products that they find online that are in direct competition with the products of their clients. Besides consumer electronics, which constitutes 60 percent of Loomis's business, the company's primary clients are pharmaceutical companies. Increasingly, counterfeit pharmaceuticals are edging into the market. (According to the *Washington Post*, counterfeit drugs account for an 8 percent chunk of the $32 billion worldwide prescription drug market.) If cease-and-desist letters don't put a stop to the illegal sales, Loomis puts in a call to his contacts at the DEA, the Secret Service, or the FBI.

In some cases, brands subsidize the police directly to better protect their "brand equity." The idea of private companies paying for police protection may sound outrageous, but foreign counterfeits have become such a problem in New York that the city actually has organized a counterfeiting task force funded in part by the brands themselves. "Members" pay $3,500 in return for the task force's services in busting counterfeiters. When the money runs out, the police can request more. Not surprisingly, the

Net Enforcers was acquired by identity management firm Intersections, Inc., in November 2007.

luxury brands pay up. In one recent example in Manhattan's notorious "Counterfeit Alley," thirty-three companies joined forces to fund a police sting on a downtown warehouse full of knockoff goods. The companies picked up the tab for twenty-four-hour surveillance of the area, nine tractor-trailers, two hundred thousand evidence bags, and the tape to seal them—not to mention the pizza and coffee delivered to the crime scene.[4]

Additionally, dozens of industries are battling their own distributors' in-house labels. Modern private-label or retailers' house brands—those store-made, formerly "generic," value-oriented, also-ran products—are more appealing and of better quality than ever before. For the past decade, global sales of private-label goods, from shampoo to cereal, have been growing at twice the rate of name brands.[5] Home Depot has a dozen different house brands selling for less than the category-leading brands, from Hampton Bay light fixtures to Behr paints. Whole Foods has a house brand in every aisle: "pantry staples" are covered under the 365 brand, for fish there's Whole Catch, and Allegro coffee, though it may look like an independent label, is a house brand too.

Even as recently as ten years ago, most private-label goods were essentially polite, inferior knockoffs, cheap alternatives with simple packaging. Walk into any national supermarket or department store chain today and you'll find private-label brands with flashy packaging and design and quality ingredients. Like varsity athletes bumped off the starting lineup, executives at leading brands are desperate to keep their standing in the market against products that offer a cheaper alternative to virtually identical goods.

And better doesn't always beat cheaper. Ol' Roy dog food, Wal-Mart's bargain-priced in-house brand (named after founder Sam Walton's hunting companion), currently dominates the pet food category as the number-one-selling brand in the United States, despite the fact that Wal-Mart, which doesn't promote the brand, is up against expensive marketing campaigns from boutique and mainstream dog-food brands.[6] Wal-Mart carries dozens of other private-label brands, from EverStart car batteries and Mainstays curtains to Get It Together couches and Spring Valley vitamins. All cost significantly less than their leading, brand-name competitors (produced, in many cases, overseas and rebranded for U.S. shelves).

□   □   □

Today's feature wars are quick, fierce, and often vastly expensive. Private-label goods are often as good as or better than brand names. The rapid influx of low-cost knockoffs from overseas leaves leading brands with little reason to break their necks trying to stay out in front of the pack. Why dump money into R&D for an uncertain, expensive, and ultimately fleeting advantage? After all, branding is quick, easy to change, and more reliable. Spending months or years developing a new technology, revamping distribution channels, or identifying the right market segment—all for uncertain results—are tasks that aren't nearly as appealing as an image overhaul. With a tap of the branding wand, AT&T became Cingular. After a few months, Cingular morphed back into AT&T. Granted, such moves cost those particular investors at least $60 million a pop, and often A-list executives. (Mark Lefar, AT&T's CMO, retired after the flip-flop back to AT&T.) What's notable in this case, however, is that branders pulled each transition off in a matter of months. Pouring the same $120 million into research with the risk of nothing to show for it after years of work is a tough sell for the short-tenured executive core.

Some companies run out of ideas and are forced to trade in on their brand name, selling T-shirts to pad the bottom line. Others cut corners, slapping their brand on cheaper and cheaper products, selling little more than the name until the equity of the name is compromised. Levi jeans, Elizabeth Arden, Tommy Hilfiger—all have launched low-cost lines at Wal-Mart in recent years. Famous designers like Isaac Mizrahi, Todd Oldam, and Oscar de la Renta are producing clothes for Target and Dillard's. Some call this diluting the brand—others prefer "design slumming." While the short-term results have generally been favorable for consumers, producing lesser-quality goods for less money floods the market with cheap excess—such as "disposable" clothing and an endless parade of "limited edition" products doomed to the discount rack.

Rather than innovate, many brands are resorting to other attention-getting strategies like "broadening the brand promise" and launching brand extensions (the use of a known brand name on a new product—such as Swiffer, Swiffer WetJet, Swiffer Sweeper, and so on). In light of this trend, many are questioning how long the United States will remain the world's most innovative nation.

The CEO and president of the American Management Association (AMA), Edward Reilly, and his 700,000 constituents around the world make up the world's leading membership-based management development organization. At last count, the AMA provides management training, educational courses, and seminars to 486 of the Fortune 500 companies. From his vantage point, Reilly sees innovation in U.S. companies dwindling. Because American companies have been so successful in the past, many, according to him, are becoming complacent.

Reilly raised the flag in 2006, when the AMA published an exhaustive global study on innovative practices in businesses around the world. (The AMA has offices in thirteen countries besides the United States.) The study, "The Quest for Innovation: A Global Study in Innovation Management, 2006–2016," disclosed that while more than two-thirds of U.S. businesses considered innovation important, fewer than one-third actually had any processes in place to oversee and manage results.[7]

Though it's difficult to believe in the context of today's fickle stock market, the AMA found that companies that devote more time, money, and attention to innovation—something that can make impatient shareholders antsy—actually end up offering a greater degree of satisfaction to their shareholders. Findings consistently indicated a "high corollary" between brands that took a more serious approach to innovation and brands that offered shareholders a return on their investment. More troubling was what the AMA saw elsewhere in the world: widespread enthusiasm for systemizing innovation, formalizing the process, and measuring results.

This isn't to imply that U.S. businesses are disinclined to systems or formal processes. It's just that they're focusing on branding over innovation. Branding firms spend vast amounts of time and ingenuity developing programs such as LPK's "Tool Box Vision," Landor's "BrandAsset Valuator," and Interbrand's "Brand Equity Model." In turn, companies devote significant resources to implementing these plans in time to meet rapid product cycles. There's just no time or money for ambitious innovation.

Other groups have joined the AMA in sounding the alarm bells over R&D in the United States. The 2008 Global R&D Report estimates that China and India will match that of the United States within the next decade. The Task Force on the Future of American Innovation (TFFAI), a Washington, D.C., outfit, determined that U.S. companies upped their total R&D by 43 percent between 1995 and 2005. During the same period, however, China, Ireland, Israel, Singapore, South Korea, and Taiwan collectively grew R&D investments by 214 percent—almost five times the rate of the United States. Few of the TFFAI's other recent metrics are heartening. The U.S. share of global high-tech exports shrank by nearly half between 1980 and 2003, and American universities graduate just two-thirds of the world average of science and engineering students (measured as a percentage of all graduates).

In keeping with the trend, the United Nations' most recent "International Labor Review," released in September 2007, found that while Americans are still the most productive workers in the global economy, they continue to work less each year.[8] The average U.S. worker clocked 1,804 hours in 2006, 30 less than in 2000. By comparison, workers in South Korea, Bangladesh, Sri Lanka, Hong Kong, China, Malaysia, and Thailand all put in over 2,200 average hours per worker.

◻   ◻   ◻

Most companies rely on outside branding firms to over-think things for them. And with so many schools of thought about branding, it's often difficult to determine what, if anything, separates good from bad branding. "We continually find that people don't even know the questions they should be asking," sighs LPK's Recker. (This isn't too much of a concern, of course, if you're making up the answers.)

What executives do know is that everyone else seems to be doing it. In some ways, this gulf of knowledge resembles the relationship between car owners and their mechanics. And like auto work, every town has its overpriced high-end shops and its small-time operators.

Even after a multimillion-dollar redesign of a product, consumers often don't notice a difference. Back at LPK, Recker flips between before-and-after shots of a rebranding project for Hershey's Kisses. The new package looks pretty much like the old package (the candy was unchanged). "Consumers are not going to recognize that this is a radical shift in what their trusted Kisses is all about." Recker grins as he brings up the next slide. "Look between the K and the I," he says, almost furtively. After a moment, there it is—a silhouette embedded in the capital K, puckered lips. It's a cute flourish, evocative of the arrow hidden in the FedEx logo.

Many branders have a hard time proving the impact of their work. Leading me through slides of LPK's work on Valvoline motor oil, Recker demonstrates that the firm's branders didn't just futz with the logo or the advertising; they reshaped the physical dimensions of the product itself, giving it a high-shouldered bottle—"so it looks more proud." "Even if it's 'perceived functionality,'" says Recker with the utmost seriousness, "you win. Consumers don't really know that." Maybe. Sales may jump with the introduction of a new bottle, label, or buzzword, but these aesthetic cues only carry the illusion so far. Ultimately, consumers will recognize when one product isn't as good as another.

□   □   □

Again and again, I observed the *Groundhog Day* phenomenon—the same clients boasted about at one branding firm in the morning (their redesigned logos hanging from banners or engraved on plaques) being rebranded at a different firm in the afternoon. Like a mad game of musical chairs, brands hop from one firm to the next. Frequent leadership changes at the brands themselves play no small part in the confusion.

After handing its brand over to FRCH for a total overhaul, Linens 'n Things vanished from the firm's client list. "We did a lot of work with them," says Kevin Dugan, director of marketing. "But the team we worked with is all gone now." Deskey had just completed a total redesign of the Brawny paper towel brand (according to one executive, the old Brawny man "looked like a seventies porn star") when the brand's manufacturer, Georgia-Pacific, was acquired by another company. Deskey's contact at Brawny was gone. The firm ran into a similar problem with L'Oreal. Even after Deskey doubled the brand's kids' shampoo sales at Wal-Mart (and dressed up a staffer in a cartoon-fish costume, one of the company's mascots), L'Oreal trotted off to a new brander.

Inevitably, this constant flipping from one branding shop to another creates considerable confusion, straining traditional business channels. Disconnected from the branding frenzy back in Cincinnati, employees in the field will occasionally call one firm only to find that their brand has moved on.

The constant churn is amplified by the fact that Procter & Gamble, in an effort to keep its employees engaged and to broaden their experience, transfers brand managers regularly among its hundreds of brands. When a new brand manager is rotated in, inevitably the rebranding process is again put in motion. Because top execs tend to focus on the billion-dollar brands, the smaller brands provide a sandbox for newer brand managers to learn the ropes. A common result is the creation of a series of line extensions as managers look to boost revenues and get promoted. As long as the sales are growing, no one pays too much attention.

□   □   □

In a race for mind-share, some companies are consolidating their resources under fewer labels and hoping to leverage a few choice brand names capable of breaking through the clutter. Unilever, Procter & Gamble's primary competitor in the consumer packaged goods business, has pared hundreds of brands from its product lineup— from about sixteen hundred brands in 2000 to just four hundred today.[9] The logic behind this strategy is shaky:

fewer brands allow broader brand promises. Overextending the brand, however, requires that companies effectively assume more space in the consumer's life by rooting the brand even deeper. The result of so many broadened promises and ambitious extensions is a baffled, if not bemused, customer.

Today we can purchase a ridiculous array of products inspired by brand extremism: Ferrari-brand computers, Play-Doh–brand scented perfume, *Chicken Soup for the Soul*–brand pet food. The trend has even inspired annual awards for the worst brand extensions. Corralled by New York branding firm Tipping Sprung and selected by hundreds of marketing professionals, past winners include Harley-Davidson–brand cake decorating kits and Cheetos-brand lip balm.

Understandably, brand extensions often lead to heated debate within the branding community. "The difference between Interbrand and a lot of other branding firms around town is we're not just a bunch of whores who will do whatever a company says," says Todd Sebastian, formerly the chief account officer for Interbrand.

When the brand managers for PUR—Procter & Gamble's answer to the Brita water filtration brand—approached Sebastian with the plan for a new PUR pitcher with flavor buttons, he was conflicted. PUR was, after all, about selling clean water, not Kool-Aid. Interbrand ultimately worked up a concept for PUR, but Sebastian turned down any further work on the brand. "If you look at the package they forced us into creating, nothing says filtered. All you see is this wash of raspberries. This is exactly what you shouldn't do; it undermines the brand and confuses the customer." (PUR launched its "Flavor Options" line in May 2007.)

The impact of short tenures and the pursuit of short-term results can be felt in almost every industry. Such is the case that those stubborn companies that insist on building their brand the old-fashioned way—by consistently producing a product people like—stand out more than ever before. With upward of 1,000 stores, Spanish clothing retailer Zara pulled down $7.6 billion in revenues in 2006, while devoting just 0.3 percent to advertising.[10] The company was number 64 in Interbrand's 2007 global brand rankings, landing in front of Rolex (number 71), Motorola (number 77), and Prada (number 99).

Zara's success is the result of good designs, inexpensive materials, and an impressive supply chain. The company designs and manufactures its own clothes and rarely franchises. In contrast, Gap (number 61) spends hundreds of millions each year promoting its brands with MP3 giveaways and pitches by celebrities like John Mayer, Lucy Lui, and Sarah Jessica Parker.

Chelsea Milling Company has made few changes to the packaging on its well-known Jiffy mix boxes in more than fifty years, yet generations of consumers have returned to the same familiar blue packages. Though the company has never advertised, it dominates the muffin mix category with an expected 55 percent market share by unit sales, accounting for estimated sales of $62 million a year. Betty Crocker and Pillsbury have spent decades and untold millions trying to steal some of Jiffy's market share.

On the Internet, Google provides superlative search technology, endless email storage, intuitive online calendars, and dozens upon dozens of other services at no cost. And while the company sells advertising to more than 300,000 companies, it spends just a tiny fraction of its revenues on its own advertising.

In-N-Out Burger is another iconic brand that rarely advertises or speaks to the press. ("We never want to seem as though we are seeking publicity," explained one spokesperson years ago.) The chain, with an estimated $217 million in revenues, has been putting the rest of the fast-food industry to shame for years. Its brand recipe is a simple menu, great food, and no heat lamps. Strong sales have spurred the chain to expand throughout California, Arizona, and Nevada. McDonald's spent an estimated $1.7 billion in 2006 on advertising in the United States alone, amounting to about one day's worth of sales more per store than In-N-Out. (In-N-Out stores would likely have outsold their McDonald's counterparts, but they close their doors on Thanksgiving and Christmas.)

What unifies these companies isn't their disdain for advertising, but their initiative in delivering a high-quality product that people like, at good value. Successful, enduring brands are either truly innovative and outstanding or a great value. They have never needed much advertising. They don't have to reinvigorate their employees with brand-morale building or rely shamelessly on empty company taglines. Their products fulfill the legitimate purpose of the brand. For those that don't—and with the rise of competitors both foreign and domestic, corporate insecurity is widespread in the current market—branding, rebranding, and cobranding are the answers.

In many cases, companies are so desperate to launch a new product that entire brands are imagined and designed in just days. The fastest billion-dollar brand in Procter & Gamble history, Swiffer, the cleaning wand with a disposable pad, was "the goose that laid a golden egg," according to Don Childs of laga, and one that offered an inspiration to brands far and near. As the branding firm responsible for the launch, laga found itself in an awkward position. Execs were proud of their success, but Procter & Gamble was asking them to extend the Swiffer name at a breakneck pace. With sales of the original product soaring—and its appearance everywhere from *Saturday Night Live* to the cover of *Rolling Stone*—Procter & Gamble immediately started exploring ways to capitalize on the Swiffer name. Besides the standard Swiffer Sweeper, customers can now choose from the X-

Large Sweeper, the Duster, the WetJet, the SweeperVac, the CarpetFlick, and more.

What the best branders realize is that broadening the promise and extending the brand will only get brands so far. We live in a cluttered media environment where the consumer's attention is a precious resource. It's no longer enough to sell an innovative feature or project an image, as brands have done for hundreds of years. Entire industries are rapidly being commoditized by easily replicable digital technology, the rise in quality private-label goods, and the influx of cheap competitors from Asia. Innovation, quickly copied, no longer wins the day. To make matters worse, brands must court an increasingly fickle and jaded consumer inundated by choice. Niche products abound, but fleetingly, appearing only momentarily on retail shelves. It's not just NASCAR M&Ms, it's Band-Aids in an array of hues to match every skin tone, and it's Tide with Downy in a limited-edition scent. With so many niche products breaking consumers up into smaller and smaller groups, brands can discontinue any one product in order to launch another without disappointing too many people at a time. The game has changed: the world is in fact flat, and so is the global playing field.

Facing these challenges, branders have come to understand that in some cases it takes more than a patina of "perceived functionality" to convince consumers to buy brand-name products. To continue to capture our loyalty and demand a premium price, companies must reach beyond the shelf and find new ways to develop and extend their brands. They must control more than the logo, the bottle, or the mission statement—they must control the brand experience.

THREE

Buying Our Way into
Being

We didn't set out . . . to start a religion.
BMW television advertisement, 2007

From "the long tail" and "trading up" to "the paradox of choice" and "the Wal-Mart effect," globalization and the Internet have spawned a series of peculiar consumer behaviors and corresponding business theories. With each evolution of the market, brands have scrambled to refine their appeals and anchor themselves as deeply as possible in consumers' minds. Considering that, on average, people fulfill 80 to 85 percent of their needs with just 150 everyday items, brands are in a tough spot.[1] With such fierce competition for so little space, brands are forced to strategize on how best to bond with consumers.

Out of this frenzy, a small movement of experiential marketers has been gathering momentum. Hailing the dawn of the "experience economy," they describe their work as "making meaning" and "guiding transformations." Some resemble the patent medicine salesmen of the nineteenth century, ready to take the show on the road. Others busy themselves with publishing reams of complex charts and diagrams from ivory towers. Their common ground lies in a desire to create and manage branded experiences, branded memories, and branded emotional connections.

Experiences open up emotional shortcuts, and the brain acts three thousand times faster than normal when stimulated by emotion.[2] Even the drabbest brands are seeking ways to infuse emotion into their products. But in practice, experiential marketing is far from simple. While some goods naturally lend themselves to developing emotional bonds with consumers—cars and luxury handbags among them—others are forced to devise new ways to connect.

For the average customer, price is a rational purchasing consideration and brand an emotionally driven one. Nowhere is this more obvious than in the toilet paper aisle, where dozens of brands offer virtually the same product. Dwarfed by an eight-foot tall, one-hundred-foot long wall of relative sameness, customers rarely rely on powerful emotions or memories when making their choice. Unless, that is, they've danced with the Charmin bear.

□   □   □

John Baker chuckles, recalling people's reactions to Potty Palooza, Charmin's twenty-seven-room deluxe traveling bathroom facility. Painted sky-blue with fluffy white clouds, latched to the bed of an eighteen-wheeler, the massive mobile commode inspires awe when it rolls up to its temporary home on Baker's plot in Mansfield, Indiana, for the annual ten-day Covered Bridge Festival. The high-end stalls have become so popular with visitors that many will walk a half-mile and wait in a fifteen-minute line, passing vacant portable toilets along the way.

While you may not have heard of Charmin's traveling toilet, those who have experienced it rarely forget the dancing Charmin bear, the TV-equipped luxury stalls, or the aromatherapy. This kind of brand recognition (for toilet paper) is something that companies are just beginning to grasp.

During the late summer of 2000, Ohio residents cozied up to Procter & Gamble's Charmin bath tissue when the brand sponsored a set of toilets at the State Fair. Claiming that sales saw a bump, Procter & Gamble decided to take the show on the road, and Potty Palooza was born.[3]

Most consumer products companies can get away with dropping small samples in the mail—high on cost, low on imagination, and famously inefficient. Mailing an entire roll of tissue has never been an option, and sending out a four-sheet trial pack of toilet paper just doesn't cut it. But in taking on the challenge they faced getting their product into customers' hands, Charmin execs devised a branding legend.

Complete with flushing porcelain toilets, hardwood floors, and air conditioning, Potty Palooza gets little competition from the ranks of rented porta-potties lined up outside the concerts, sporting events, and festivals it frequents.

Since its debut in 2002, the Palooza truck has been on the road as much as eleven months a year, visiting twenty-six to thirty events annually, from the Super Bowl to the Arizona Hot-Air Balloon Festival. In light of its success, Procter & Gamble has added a smaller, twelve-stall truck (Potty Palooza number 2) and developed similar traveling shows for Crest Toothpaste and the Gillette Fusion Razor. (Crest's eighteen-wheeler offers "brushing stations," complete with scents and music, inside a forty-eight-foot truck in the shape of a tube of toothpaste; the Fusion tractor-trailer is less dramatic.) Potty Palooza travels to nearly half the states in the United States and includes several stops in Canada. To maximize the brand's exposure, Charmin's road team tries to target new locations each year, but events aimed at mothers with children take priority.

"Guests" at Potty Palooza are offered a menu of TP options that go beyond the standard white roll, with features that appeal to customers' sense of smell and touch—a multisensory experience. A selection of offerings from years past includes Charmin Ultra (the brand's premium offering, upgraded in 2000 and standard on the tour), Charmin Plus (with chamomile), Charmin Aloe and E, and Charmin Scents—with perfumes like Wildflower Fresh and Shower Fresh built into the roll. (One line boasted a limited-edition fall holiday scent.) All told, Charmin's five million annual guests use some ten thousand cushioned rolls—enough to necessitate a separate supply truck in the Potty Palooza caravan.

In the language of experiential marketing, that's not a line of people waiting out front, it's a captive audience. As guests wait, they take part in the full branding experience. The Charmin bear keeps crowds busy by teaching the Charmin dance to people in line, while a team of branding reps freshen stalls and direct visitors in and out. At the Mansfield Covered Bridge Festival, which attracts one and a half to two million visitors, it can mean cleaning up after five thousand guests a day and emptying "black water" five to ten times.

John Baker and his wife Debbie, who lease their land to festival vendors each year, could be earning themselves an extra $10,000 by leasing out the quarter-acre occupied by Charmin to other vendors. But the Bakers have proudly hosted the truck for free year after year because it's good for business. Before Potty Palooza, the Bakers kept 70 percent of their clients from year to year and space went begging. Today 90 percent of their vendors return and there's not a vacant lot in sight. But the truck's annual return owes itself to more than the Bakers' bottom line. After Potty Palooza made its first appearance at the overcrowded festival in 2002, thirty thousand people signed a petition to bring it back.

Though the truck is "not currently touring," according to Charmin's website, the Potty Palooza concept has been so successful—purportedly boosting Charmin sales by 14 percent—that Procter & Gamble opened a storefront Palooza location in New York's ultra-high-rent Times Square, staffed by Charmin crew dressed as toilets, during the 2006 and 2007 holiday season.

The cumulative effect of Charmin's campaign has been to celebrate a highly private activity. By redefining a visit to the toilet as a commercially viable branding opportunity, Charmin has placed its brand squarely between public and private life. Such is the objective of the ambitious brands of our day—to expand the limits of what is acceptable, leave a mark on fresh turf, and insinuate themselves into the fabric of our waking lives.

❑   ❑   ❑

Away from the cold and rainy spring streets of Montreal, Darrel Rhea is basking in the warm glow of minor celebrity. Standing at the podium at the Design Management Institute's eighteenth annual Corporate/Brand Identity Conference, Rhea is at the peak of his career. The CEO of Cheskin, a respected marketing and branding firm and, today, the keynote speaker at the premier conference of the branding industry, he waits patiently for the applause to subside after his introduction. Rhea looks the part of the design guru—sports jacket, bold, angular glasses, his thinning hair close-cut. Beaming confidently at the room full of designers, copywriters, and self-styled branding coaches and consultants, he is clearly adored. "It's like coming back to summer camp!" he shouts, and the crowd—excited, almost anxious—laughs with him.

Rhea has come to the subterranean ballroom beneath the Marriott Chateau Champlain to outline a brief history of branding and to proclaim his ambitious vision for its future. By Rhea's math, the modern era of branding began in the late nineteenth and early twentieth centuries with the "economic experience" (Procter & Gamble, Ford, Edison): price and value were customers' prime consideration. Rhea outlines the development of product demand, the era of so-called functional experience, when product innovations brought us better features—more flavors, more colors, more styles. Next were the "emotional" and "identity" phases: marketers leveraged social research and broadcast media to manufacture the desires of mid-twentieth-century suburban families. The final phase, in which brands aim to sculpt the very ways we think about ourselves, is about making meaning. Perched above the rows and rows of branders absorbing his every word, Rhea knows he's preaching to the choir. Nowhere will he find an audience more eager or more receptive.

Rhea is one of many people in the branding community who increasingly sees brands as the arbiters of meaning in our lives. For a brand to be a success, it must capitalize on the organic underpinnings of the human experience—community, relationships, and values—in an effort to create meaning.

Today's consumers are inundated with opportunities to personalize every facet of their lives, from TiVo to customized sneakers to M&Ms printed with personalized messages to cellular ring tones to suit every musical taste. Twenty years ago, buying a Ford F150 involved choosing from a handful of colors, engines, and flat-bed options. There are now literally hundreds of options to choose from—a rainbow of colors and multiple cab lengths and features like power-folding heated signal mirrors with puddle lamps, a reverse sensing system, and power moonroofs. Even a Harley-Davidson-branded F150 is available. But is buying and owning an F150 today any more meaningful than it was in the past? Do more options reinforce the modern customer's sense of identity? And if more options don't add meaning, what else will?

Promoted by Rhea and his colleagues, the tactical shift toward "owning" meaning, experience, and identity has gathered momentum across the branding industry in the past several years. Clicking the remote, Rhea pulls up a slide outlining human values—conduits of meaning from which he believes brands can benefit. Oneness, brotherhood, beauty, truth, wonder, accomplishment, security, freedom, justice, love, duty, wisdom. . . . Row upon row of pens and pencils scribble to keep up.

Darrel Rhea is large in every sense—in his size, his confidence, and his ideas. Standing upwards of six-foot-four, he towers over the patient circles of admirers that pool at his side as he works the room. Bow-tied waiters in white dinner jackets refresh trays of hors d'oeuvres while a trio of musicians in French-inspired clothing play Frank Sinatra. The accordion, muffled by the barroom's heavy curtains and carpeting, sounds out of place amid the sharply dressed design mavens. Yet, disguised as a French theater with a stage recessed below a tiered sitting area, the bar is an appropriate setting for a crowd of high-powered creators of commercial reality.

While brands have been consciously and cleverly helping us shape our sense of self for years, the psychology, tools, and tactics behind those efforts are improving faster than ever. The advances afford us more enriching brand experiences, but can our minds stay one step ahead of the marketing? And what does it mean when our sense of "meaning" and our sense of "identity" are shaped by someone trying to sell us something?

Diamonds, for one, play a fairly "meaningful" role in most Americans' lives: 80 percent of brides in the United States receive a diamond engagement ring before they get married.[4] We can trace the significance of the diamond in American history to the 1930s and 1940s, when the De Beers Company launched an aggressive national campaign to bring attention to its product. Between 1939 and 1979, wholesale diamond sales grew from $21 million to $2.1 billion.[5] (Marketers even tried—unsuccessfully—to get men to wear diamond engagement rings.) De Beers was neither the first nor the last corporation to engender meaning through marketing. Hallmark has been criticized for years for popularizing and profiting from any number of so-called Hallmark holidays, such as "Christmas in July" or "Boss's Day."

Recently, brands in just about every industry have started rallying behind social causes and tapping into a sense of meaning and community. Though not a new idea, cause branding has grown exponentially in recent years as more companies have recognized the advantages of social responsibility. Unilever's Dove soap has gotten behind the American Cancer Society, and Procter & Gamble's Mr. Clean has a community outreach program that encourages consumers to pick up around their neighborhood and "give your community a thorough clean."

Tapping into customer identity has always been a principal means of selling products. In the past, brands largely appealed to customers by employing images or words that resonated with their sense of self—or a sense of self that they aspired to. As Niki Fitzgerald, creative director of graphic design at the Cincinnati-based architectural branding firm FRCH, sees it, "People choose brands because they make them feel good about themselves. They're aligning their values."

If brands are here to help us align our values, then the role of the modern branding professional is to amplify those aspirational values in the design and packaging of the product. The better things look—be they packs of gum or luxury sedans—the more people will desire them. Designers love this axiom because it implies that, if the design is good enough, the product is less important in the overall equation. We are, effectively, positioning ourselves with our purchases and buying our way into being.

According to the branders of Luvs diapers at Deskey in Cincinnati, you can understand mothers through the diapers they purchase. Branding specialists at Deskey, which won Procter & Gamble's "First Moment of Truth" award two years in a row, had to closely examine the competition's appeal when they were strategizing for the Luvs campaign.* Up against industry leaders like Pampers and Huggies, Luvs is, as one brander put it, "the red-headed, ugly adopted stepchild" of diaper brands. Distinguishing Luvs from the competition meant taking advantage of an opening.

"Pampers are all about the mom," Doug Sovonick, Deskey's chief creative officer, explains. "The images show the mom doting over the baby—they say, 'We are doing this. Are you a good mom too?" Huggies, in contrast, focuses on the child. With a less expensive brand on their hands, Deskey aimed to keep the imagery simple

---

*The "moment of truth" refers to the critical point when customers first engage a product in a store setting.

and unpretentious. "We might show a dad or a sibling in there. The message is intended to be *real*: 'Life is more important than what brand of diaper you buy.'" That's the overt message at least. The subtext is just the opposite.

Most consumers today are savvy enough to understand that identity and status figure into even the most irrelevant purchases. No one *really* believes that buying a bottle of Joy or Cheer will result in experiencing those actual feelings. If there's a cheaper bottle on a lower shelf, most customers will opt for saving money.

Losing traction with consumers, brands are investing in marketing methods that go beyond aspirational imagery. To do so, branders are capitalizing on some age-old tricks of the trade.

□   □   □

Since 1972, academic researchers around the country have conducted the General Social Survey (GSS). Measuring socioeconomic status, family characteristics, race relations, and morality issues, the GSS operates like a social barometer of our times. In 1985 the GSS asked participants to number their "close friends." Respondents were likely to claim three—often noting that these relationships were based in their neighborhood or local community. In 2006 the *American Sociological Review* published the survey's most recent findings, which showed a threefold increase over the past two decades in the number of

Americans who didn't have anyone with whom to discuss important matters. Specifically, the GSS found that nearly one-quarter of the 1,500 participants claimed they had no confidants at all. Half acknowledged having two or fewer close friends.[6]

Americans are in effect getting lonelier. In 1985 the best means we had to "reach out and touch someone" was the telephone. For all the advances in communications since then—cellular phones, the Internet, instant messages, email, chat rooms, social networking sites—we now feel more isolated.

Among the more troubling findings in the most recent GSS report was that the increasingly small number of close friends in our lives is creating a vacuum and leaving us vulnerable to other influences. Brands openly acknowledge their desire to step in and fill the void. One reason for the drop in the number of close friends Americans count within their inner circle is that, rather than bringing us closer together, globalization and technology are undermining traditional forms of community. Armed with a biological imperative to form communities, we create makeshift tribes around the most widely recognized and readily available icons. The resulting "brand tribes," as French marketing professor Bernard Cova has described them, act as surrogates for the communities partially eroded and disbanded by the introduction of the cellular phone and the Internet and by the resulting decrease in face-to-face communication.

Hungry for community, we're turning to brands. After home and work, Starbucks is the "third place." Much of Apple's brand cache stems from the sense of belonging that loyalists describe. Naturally, brands are happy to help with community, acting as warm gathering places where people with mutual interests can share common experiences and a sense of togetherness. In turn, brands assume their place as institutions residing at the heart of our culture, taking responsibility for helping to establish and maintain traditions, values, and measures of status. Strong brands attract like-minded people interested in belonging ("The Choice of a New Generation"), status ("The Ultimate Driving Machine"), personal traits ("Ford Tough"), or philosophy ("Think Different," "Just Do It"). It isn't just by purchasing brands that we become part of the brand community; we talk brand jive.

We become brand citizens when our collective exposure to branding affords us brand language—a kind of brand shorthand. Corporations communicate with us through brands, and we communicate with each other through our brand choices. This is because modern brands denote so much more than quality or price. The statement "I shop at Target" implies a different worldview than "I shop at Wal-Mart." While they cost the same amount of money, a Mexican-made Dodge means something entirely different than a Honda made in Tennessee. More than any single political or religious affiliation, purchases reflect the decisions that most clearly define us today.

What better route to community and identity than shared language, rituals, and experience? With each waking moment, we define ourselves through our experiences—who we talk to, where we go, what we buy. Experiences represent multisensory gold mines for brands, trapdoors into our most deeply held beliefs and values.

For some consumers, the shared brand experience offers more value than the product itself. Experiences translate into memories, and in an economy where so much is disposable, good ones are worth searching out. "Experiences are better than durable goods," says Harvard psychology professor Daniel Gilbert, author of *Stumbling into Happiness*. "Experiences don't hang around long enough to disappoint you. What you have left are wonderful memories."[7]

Authors of marketable aspirations and mythology, brands are experts at mirroring our idealized lives. Modern brand tribes are bound by a shared sense of connection rather than a real-world, physical community of neighbors. As long as brand rituals and cult objects continue to generate a common attraction, the sense of connection is maintained. Once the buyer's remorse sets in, however, the tribe loses a member. Relationships brokered by brands are by and large superficial. In one recent study by the Minneapolis marketing firm Yamamoto

Moss, only 16 percent of marketers believed that brands make life more meaningful.

No matter how ephemeral, with shared experiences comes a sense of community. With the resources and initiative to fill the void, brands are rushing to frame the communities of tomorrow. Materially linked to a tribe of like-minded enthusiasts, the owner of a Harley-Davidson edition F150 truck feels a sense of belonging, but will he feel more?

For most of us, the idea of a branded object eclipsing the bonds of family, friendship, work, or spirituality is ludicrous. But branding's most fervent gurus celebrate the best brands for their capacity to establish themselves firmly in our hearts and minds. Our relationships with our dearest brands, they argue, ought to resonate on a spiritual level. To this end, one branding strategy that has gained momentum in the past few years is the concept of the "brand church"—places of "worship" for brand tribes to gather.

◻   ◻   ◻

"Experience started to really pick up as we came up against the limitations of marketing and design in branding," says Rhea. "[Customers are] experiencing things we cannot influence." In an effort to better manage brand experiences, branders recognize that the best way to control the perception of a product is to own and control the environment. In recent years, brands that never imagined engaging the consumer face to face are paying rent for retail space that offers an opportunity for real-time, real-world interaction.

A brand church, much like a traditional retail space, is defined by its architecture, rituals, and representatives. But in the elevated showcase, products are defined by a grander experience—one that taps into our sensory landscape through smells, sounds, and texture. The evolution of the brand church has not been forced upon consumers by overzealous brands. It is the logical extension of our attachment to the products with which we identify.

Borrowing from religion, brands are cherry-picking rituals to forge stronger brand identities. To a degree, this comes in response to shoppers who increasingly demand moral fiber and civic values from brands—outward expressions of positive endorsements, charity campaigns, or ethically rigorous business practices. The pinnacle of brand exposure is the hallowed space of the brand church. The most sophisticated brands "are those that not only anchor themselves in tradition but also adopt religious characteristics."[8] It's not much of a stretch to think of a few brand messiahs. Microsoft has Bill Gates (saving the world and passing the collection plate), Omnimedia has Martha (risen from the dead), and Apple has Steve Jobs (the second coming). Emanating a near-pope-like aura, Oprah counsels her subjects on everything from politics to personal values. Other brands have been following suit.

In the late 1990s, sites like Amazon.com and eBay.com proved that companies didn't need a storefront to develop a blockbuster business model. Some brands even abandoned their street addresses for URLs, opting to save money on labor and real estate by operating entirely online. But lately, brands that would seem to have no business paying for a lease are opening their doors to consumers. *Wired*, a business magazine that made its name championing the World Wide Web as the logical evolution of all commerce, recently opened a physical store in New York. Devoted to expensive gadgets and offering "the feel of a gallery," the *Wired* store offers its customers everything from cell phones to high-tech teddy bears.

News Corp's Fox brand has both sports grills and convenience stores, and ESPN has a chain of "all encompassing sports dining and entertainment Mecca[s] where guests are immersed in an ESPN experience." None are franchised outside the company's control. NASCAR has its own "Thunder" stores, "designed to emphasize the NASCAR brand" with "an unconventional use of logo and multimedia . . . a variety of decorative materials and thematic components," according to Bullock, Smith & Partners, the architects involved.

ESPN's decision to sell onion rings and chicken wings is a manifestation of the larger imperative to bring people "inside" the brand and immerse them in a controlled sensory environment. In such a managed space, a homogenized, prepackaged experience with the brand lets customers partake in a shared brand story. Ideally, such experiences grow the brand community. Granted, this approach isn't fail-safe. Much was made of computer manufacturer Gateway's ill-fated foray into retail spaces. In its 1997 annual report, Gateway proudly hailed its "Country Stores"—decked out in an unmistakable Holstein patchwork—as a means of communicating the company's "culture and roots"; Gateway claimed that the comfortable farm decor offered a low-stress environment in which to shop for technology.

In the end, Gateway's Country Stores failed miserably. Retailers didn't like them because they had to compete with the company on the ground. After a halfhearted attempt to sell TVs and DVD players, the entire herd (three hundred worldwide) of black-and-white cow-patterned Country Stores was shut down in 2004, eight years after the first store opened.

But many companies, in the belief that Gateway had the right idea, are creating spaces that operate more like retail sanctuaries than stores. Prada set a new standard for retail in 2001 when it moved into the space formerly occupied by a branch of the Guggenheim Museum. Its $40

million Rem Koolhaas–designed Manhattan store represented a massive investment of capital for a showcase
space—dominated by black and white, with stark, boxy
lines and semitransparent walls—that elevated luxury
clothing and accessories to a new level. Launching its retail
stores the same year, Apple now has nearly two hundred locations around the world. According to a January 2008 estimate by Toni Sacconaghi of Bernstein Research, Apple
stores generate sales of nearly $4,500 per square foot—
more than Tiffany & Co. and Coach combined.[9] Apple's retail success stems in part from how it displays its products:
being positioned on stark altars and under spotlights ele-
vates the prestige of already popular items like the iPod
(over 100 million sold to date).

A cathedral among churches, Apple's Fifth Avenue flagship store opened in 2006 to lines around the block.
Capped by a massive clear cube, it employs a small army of
three hundred people and features a cylindrical glass elevator (designed by Steve Jobs). Descending below the
hubbub of midtown Manhattan to a ten-thousand-square-
foot brand sanctum, the elevator opens to a Bauhaus-like
white space that calls to mind the company's ubiquitous
white plastic iPods. Apple loyalists flocked to the store
during its first few months, some making pilgrimages from
around the country to line up for the grand opening, and
it has continued to draw in crowds of new converts.

"Retail is showroom," says FRCH's CCO, Paul Lech-
leiter. FRCH specializes in branded spaces. "Apple started

that. Dell is doing that. Nokia is doing it. It's about the social event, creating a variety of experiences on multiple levels." Akin to a place of worship that functions as a space apart from the outside world where the intangible values and beliefs of a particular religion are reinforced by physical elements, brand churches are the epitome of brand control. Major brands are betting a lot of money that having more control will translate into more profit.

The better you can control the environment, the more you'll sell. It's a formulaic approach to retail, though the tangible elements of a brand's retail environment are often as memorable as the product. (Think, for example, of the sounds of various electronics demonstration stations throughout a Best Buy, or the smell of new sneakers in a Foot Locker.) In the future, some branders boast that brand-centric locations will enhance the experience by anticipating and catering to customers' interests in a near-prescient fashion.

Late in 2005, Nokia began opening Nokia flagship stores—dubbed "experience centers"—in the top eighteen shopping districts in the world. In Nokia's Chicago experience center, designed by the same folks behind some of Apple's brand churches, the assault on the senses is all-encompassing. Bright floor-to-ceiling LED light panels mesmerize customers with a hypnotic wash of colors throughout the store. (The panels in every Nokia experience center are synchronized and controlled by Nokia engineers in London.) Rather than standard price tags, the store features digital displays and interactive kiosks packed with product information. Nokia-trained representatives—rather than the brand-agnostic third-party salespeople who broker most cell-phone sales—stand at the ready, armed with a smile. The experience centers even feature special set-aside areas, evocative of fine jewelry showrooms, to showcase phones from Nokia's boutique line of cellular phones, Vertu. Plated in gold and silver and encrusted with precious gems, a Vertu phone can sell for as much as $310,000.

The objective of such choreographed gadget worship is to create the ultimate Nokia experience—an immersive, seductive, and educational one in which every last detail embodies the Nokia brand. Days prior to the opening of its Chicago location, Nokia spokesman Keith Nowak emphasized that store's ability not just to sell phones but to engage customers on a meaningful level. "The success of this store is not predicated on sales volume, but consumer touch points," said Nowak to a reporter. "This is a brand play."[10]

□   □   □

"We infantilize customers with all play," declares James Woudhuysen, professor of forecasting and innovation at De Montfort University in the United Kingdom. The counterpoint to Darrel Rhea, who opened the DMI conference in Montreal, Woudhuysen has been invited to offer the last word. Standing before a crowd of branding acolytes, he dismisses much of the accepted doctrine.

Technology, from his perspective, is playing second fiddle to what he calls "the flashy experience." Innovation is another casualty. Not that play is all bad. "Play has its merits," he acknowledges, "but it also means losing yourself." Many customers have come to expect, even demand, losing themselves, as part of a great brand experience. Yet with brands reaching out to consumers in hopes of enriching their lives with greater meaning, overall customer satisfaction remains low.

According to a poll run by *BrandWeek*, Americans' brand expectation was up by 4.5 percent in 2006.[11] In general, we were optimistic, expressing the belief that future brands would deliver better products, services, and experiences. But branders' ability to meet our expectations had fallen 9.2 percent from the previous year. In short, we're expecting more and getting less.

Are brands failing to keep their end of the bargain, overpromising and underdelivering, or are our expectations rapidly outpacing their ability to keep up? While the former is more likely, what's important to notice is the discrepancy. If we're getting less, it seems counterintuitive that we'd continue to expect more. Our relationship with brands is, to say the least, dysfunctional.

Because not all brands can develop tactics like experiential marketing, many are opting for a more physical assault, engulfing us with brute-force advertising. They're filling our public spaces with marketing, buying their way into our entertainment, and purposefully blurring the lines between truth and advertising beyond any point of distinction. While experiential marketing may be a form of psychological warfare intended to win our hearts and minds, the invasion of branding into every corner of our environment and media is a full-on assault.

Ad
Creep

Expensive advertising courts us with hints and
images. The ordinary kind merely says, "Buy."
MASON COOLEY, *City Aphorisms*, 1994

B e it a Taco Bell promotion orchestrated by baseball
players during the 2007 World Series or an entire reality series dedicated to a brand of paper towels,
product placement (also known as brand integration or
branded entertainment) in television, film, literature, and
video games has skyrocketed in recent years. According to
the media research firm PQ Media, the estimated total
value of U.S. product placements—which is to say, the
marketing value that brands receive from such plugs—
will reach $5.5 billion in 2010. Only about one-third of
that will come with an invoice.

Product placement is both incredibly difficult to
track and fickle: it's rare to know whether or not a plug

is the result of a paid deal, a barter agreement, or pure providence. Determining who pays what in product placement is inherently vague. Naturally, some brands would prefer to keep the waters murky. (Apple has claimed that it never pays for product placement, yet it was one of the first brands in its industry to make formal inroads in Hollywood.)[1]

A cooperative partnership between a brand and a film, book, or television show has undeniable advantages. The creators of *Talladega Nights: The Ballad of Ricky Bobby*, a hokey hit comedy parodying NASCAR, claim they weren't paid to feature the brands Wonder Bread, KFC, and Old Spice throughout the film, though actors Will Ferrell and John C. Reilly wore branded racing outfits to promotional interviews on TV talk shows. In exchange for product placement, Wonder Bread promoted the film nationwide with specially printed packages of bread. In a cooperative gesture, Old Spice spent $2.3 million to help boost the movie.[2]

Such bartering is more common than one might imagine, even when promoted products aren't an obvious match for the subject matter. DHL shipping trucks in *Mission Impossible III*? Starbucks coffee in *Shrek 2*? By some accounts, all it took to land the screen time were a lot of overnight deliveries and some free java. Clearly, the concept of selling out has lost its stigma if directors are willing to donate screen time in exchange for mailing services and coffee. Hasbro marketing exec Mark Belcher didn't even get a Value Meal for cannibalizing the iconic Monopoly tokens (the hat, the dog, and so on) for brand-name products in a new version of the game released in 2006. Players can now choose from a New Balance running shoe, a Motorola phone, a pack of McDonald's French fries, a cup of Starbucks coffee, and a Toyota Prius.

In an effort to bring product placement to publishing, some companies have begun tapping authors to favorably incorporate their brands into novels. Fabula, a Russian product placement firm, brokers product placement deals with the country's leading pulp fiction and science fiction authors. For the right price, brands can buy their way into cover and title treatments. In an appeal to male customers, Electrolux commissioned a novel about men mastering the kitchen, *Men in Aprons*. Helpful housekeeping hints that strongly favor Electrolux products are littered throughout the book.[3]

Procter & Gamble made its notorious foray into publishing in 2006 when it struck a deal with the authors of *Cathy's Book* to weave Cover Girl eye shadow and lipstick into the plot of their young adult novel. In return, P&G agreed to promote the book on one of its websites. After getting wind of the book, Ralph Nader's Commercial Alert—a Washington, D.C., nonprofit agency devoted to "protecting communities from commercialism"—approached reviewers with a scathing note asking them to rely on their integrity when considering a wolf in sheep's clothing.

Well-known authors have also come under scrutiny for suspected product placement. In his recent thriller *Cross*, best-selling author James Patterson mentions the Mercedes-Benz brand nine times. His protagonist, Alex Cross, discusses the leg room in the car, the size of the sunroof, the dual-dash climate control, and what he describes as its mix of "intellect and emotion." You can almost hear the cash register ring: In an interview with *Advertising Age* nearly a year prior to publication, the general manager of Mercedes marketing communications employed the exact same phrase.[4] Contacted for a response, neither Patterson nor his publisher offered further insight into whether compensation was offered for the writer's allusions to the car.

Product placement is yet another example of branding's obsessive assault on reason—a strategy employed to slip by skeptical consumers' branding filters. Judging by how far and how fast the industry has come, our filters are already taxed to the limits. When their product-packed programs attract better ratings than their traditional rivals, media companies have little incentive to stop to consider the bombardment upon our senses of the near-constant impulse to sell.

□   □   □

When it comes to product placement and the blurring effect of the commercial influence in film and television, producer Michael Williams and his company, Scout Productions, straddle the divide between artistic integrity and full-blown obsessive branding disorder. In 2004 Williams won an Oscar for *The Fog of War*, a documentary about former defense secretary Robert S. McNamara. That same year, he also won a pair of Emmys for *Queer Eye for the Straight Guy*, a lighthearted reality TV show featuring five gay men performing lifestyle makeovers on everyday dudes.

Queer Eye* became an international hit, branching out into twenty franchises and winning Williams and his colleagues yet another Emmy the following year. Scout's employees never imagined that their off-the-wall reality makeover program, with its all-gay cast, would be such a hit. More surprising is that both *Queer Eye* and *Fog of War* emerged from the same production studio and earned top awards in their respective industries. *Fog of War* is an unflinching, unapologetic documentary. *Queer Eye* is pure fluff with product placement. Such is the unpredictable nature of the ongoing media blur, where the extremes of art and advertising emerge from two sides of the same small product studio.

"People refer to branded entertainment as the wild wild west," admits Eric Korsh, Scout's chief operating officer. "That thirty-second ad has less and less value. You have to embed the sales tool in the creative." Boasting fifteen years of experience producing commercials for

---

*The name was shortened in the third season.

brands like Nike and Blockbuster, Korsh heads up Scout's branded entertainment division, Scout Solutions.

In Korsh's opinion, using product placement rather than traditional advertising makes for a better viewing experience. Had he worked on NBC's hit show *Friends*, he would have written Ross as a Gap employee, not a pale-ontologist. "Rather than barraging viewers with a pile of ads," says Korsh, "we are providing a tacit endorsement of a lifestyle that fits a brand."

At its height, in 2004 and 2005, *Queer Eye*'s producers were receiving hundreds—and in some months often thou-sands—of unsolicited free products from companies des-perate for an on-screen endorsement from the "Fab Five." The ability to deal directly with brands rather than their media agencies made it easy for Scout to pick and choose products to put on air, exposing viewers to a wide array of unique brands. Essentially a vehicle for product placement, the show was so blatant in its promotion of goods that it would be hard to mistake any of it for subterfuge. Rarely are viewers afforded so much clarity. Brands, eager to raise their profiles in certain demographics, have but to pick the appropriate show and arrange a deal. It's not all fashion brands and soda either; even drugmakers—prohibited from advertising without mentioning side effects—are finding ways to weave their products into TV and film. Ac-cording to *Product Placement News*, pharmaceutical brands were mentioned on TV shows 462 times in 2006—twice as often as in 2004. One contraceptive brand showed up 11 times in one half-hour episode of NBC's hospital sitcom *Scrubs*. Apparently, product placement isn't just a useful tool for slipping past consumers' mental filters; it's also effective in sidestepping federal regulations.

In 2005 the European Commission announced that it would allow product placements in television, a practice previously banned across nearly all of Europe. But the European Commission mandated that notification about product placements be made at the commencement of the show—similar to the warning labels printed on cigarette and alcohol packaging. In the United States, no such regulation exists, and it's difficult to imagine anyone stepping forward to require similar methods of disclosure.

□　□　□

Scott Sturdevant is one of the few individuals who have stepped forward in an effort to curtail the steady flow of branding initiatives in the United States. The founder of Stopthelogos.com, he has spent two years protesting the gradual advance of station logos commonly found in the right corner of the screen on most television channels. In addition to static station logos, network "screen spam" comes in countless forms, from previews of upcoming shows to bright, animated ads that block large portions of programming.

DOGs (digitally originated graphics) are also known as service provider logos, insignia, artwork, obnoxicons, watermarks, snipes, and—the name most often used by the small but outspoken band of television enthusiasts who vehemently oppose them—bugs. TV enthusiasts in the United States and the United Kingdom have launched a number of petitions and websites in recent years under names like DOGwatch, Stop the TV Bugs, and The Logo-Free TV Campaign.

Networks have largely ignored the complaints. Studies reveal that most viewers don't actually mind a little on-screen branding. The truth is that we've adjusted to the bugs in the same way we've adjusted to other forms of branding. Ad creep has historically made inroads by insinuating itself, slowly but surely, into our cultural discourse in similar fashion.

From advertisements on billboards to newspaper ads, television commercials, online banners, and spam, the average American encounters between three thousand and five thousand ad messages each day, a number that has nearly tripled in the last generation. Sixty-five percent of Americans say they feel "constantly bombarded" by ads; Fifty-nine percent see ads as having little relevance to their lives.[5] Yet the ads keep coming.

Increasingly convinced of the importance of image over products and services, brands are devoting greater resources than ever before to their advertising and marketing departments. The hope is that more illusion will generate more interest, but the impact has been the opposite. Instead of learning from more messages, consumers are more often overwhelmed by information. In 2006 U.S. advertisers spent nearly $300 billion—about $10,000 a second—trying to reach us. More alarming than the annual total is the overall trend. Advertisers have spent more in the past decade than they did in the four previous decades *combined*.[6] In 1996 ad spending in the United States was estimated at $175 billion, almost half the amount of today's advertising costs.

□   □   □

With the arrival of blogs, social networking sites, globally interactive video games, and ever-expanding technology, brands are being forced to think beyond the standard thirty-second TV ad to reach their customers. As cheap mass-media advertising, democratized by the Internet and cable TV, makes it possible for even the smallest companies to reach large audiences, more and more ad clutter is generated. Each new attempt to "break through the clutter" only adds more. Extending their reach into the entertainment industry, brands are creating their own shows and video games and opening their own Hollywood studios.

Other brands resort to strong-arming tactics and subversiveness. In return for their ad dollars, some, like Bayer HealthCare, have demanded that magazines print "good news" about their products.[7] Funding for blogs, viral videos, and guerrilla advertising is similarly nebulous, and it's often impossible to distinguish brand propaganda from genuine demonstrations of customer devotion. Amid the confusion over new media, many advertisers are studying how to make use of word-of-mouth marketing, an age-old form of persuasion. Sometimes called buzz marketing, the increasingly formalized field has enlisted millions of brand-sponsored "buzz agents"—everyday folks who, in return for cash or products, will pitch items to anyone willing to listen, often without revealing their motives.

In 1965, a primetime advertisement aired on NBC, ABC, and CBS would reach 80 percent of women age 18–49 in the United States.[8] Selling was easy: companies made commercials, networks aired them, and people bought the products. Today network prime-time ratings are 40 percent lower than they were forty years ago. In 1965 a program like *Bonanza*, the western series that topped the weekly ratings, reached 32 million people. It would take two or three of today's most popular network shows to reach the same audience.

"The existing advertising paradigm sucks," lamented Michael Wiley, director of new media for General Motors' Communications Division. "It's woefully inefficient. We spend these huge dollars and we run them on television and we give the consumer very little information."[9]

The problem with commercials isn't only that they offer insufficient information, but that people have little interest in watching them in the first place. By the end of 2007, 25 million of the 100 million families in the United States had shelled out hundreds of dollars for a digital video recorder, which, like TiVo, enables them to bypass commercials altogether. Another 28 million DVRs were expected to ship worldwide in 2008.[10] Though DVR owners swear by them, the devices are wreaking havoc with TV networks and their advertisers. According to Susan Whiting, the CEO of Nielsen Media Research, their presence eliminated $600 million worth of commercials in 2007 (and at just 1.5 percent of TV advertising, it's safe to say that's a conservative estimate).

TiVo, of course, is not the sole culprit in the decline of television advertising. Today viewers have thousands of channels to choose from, leaving advertisers unsure of where to spend their dollars, while many prime-time shows are available on commercial-free DVDs or are downloadable from iTunes or YouTube.com.

□   □   □

With the arrival of digital technology, media are limited only by our imagination. We have thousands of television channels, billions of websites, tens of thousands of songs in our MP3 players, and streaming videos on our phones. But our attention is finite. Any increase in advertising inherently means less time and attention for other parts of our lives. Indeed, an economy based on attention rather than information has been gathering momentum for a decade. "What counts most is what is most scarce now, namely attention," claims Michael Goldhaber in a seminal online article, "The Attention Economy and the Net." The leading authority on the subject, Goldhaber has been writing about the attention economy since 1985. "The attention economy brings with it its own kinds of wealth," he says, "its own class divisions . . . its own forms of property."

As the novelty of each new advertising medium wears off, from ads on parking lot lines to the backs of receipts to paid space on people's foreheads, we accommodate. Naturally, advertisers accommodate too, encroaching deeper into the physical environments we inhabit. And in Goldhaber's attention economy, we can't possibly pay for it all. Even if we're just glancing for half a second (maybe enough time to absorb two or three words) at the thousands of ads we see every day on billboards, the backs of magazines, and in Web banner advertising, we are still spending thirty to sixty minutes every day noticing ads.

Locked in an escalating arms race against advertisers, telemarketers, and data harvesters, 50 million American households signed up for the Do-Not-Call Registry when it was launched in 2003—10 million of them in the first three days.[11] Today the list includes 145 million phone numbers. The Do-Not-Call Registry isn't just frustrating to telemarketers; it's also expensive: fines for companies that break the rules, such as Direct TV, have reached $5.3 million.

Abandoning telemarketing, salespeople are increasingly approaching us online with a limitless supply of banner ads, pop-ups, and spam. In 2004 Bill Gates famously declared that spam would be "solved" by 2006. Though software intended to block spam is now ubiquitous, plenty of spam manages to filter through to our in-boxes. As much as 90 percent of all email is estimated to be spam—and its overall volume is skyrocketing. According to network security firm Symantec, spam accounted for 78.5 percent of all e-mails in January 2008.[12]

Thanks to initiatives like the Do-Not-Call Registry and spam blockers, consumers do have an array of defensive options to prevent ad creep. As a result, image-centered brands are forever migrating, buying up advertising space, and promoting brands wherever space is available. Some are reconsidering traditional advertising channels and flooding them with cash and creativity. Saturated by advertising messages, we are bound to allow some to leak through the gaps in our mental filters.

□   □   □

EnVision Marketing Group is proof that no space is safe from the steady creep of sponsored messages, logos, and branding. A Little Rock–based marketing outfit, EnVision's promise is clear: to "turn unused space into new profits."

EnVision's target, though not revolutionary, is somewhat novel. First used in the mid–1960s, supermarket conveyor belts have cycled past us in utilitarian obscurity for more than four decades, waiting patiently for an enterprising soul. EnVision's main product, Ads-N-Line, is a digitally printed conveyer belt that touts full-color ads. With ten ads per belt, EnVision estimates that most customers see each ad two or three times a week. As one EnVision promotional slide put it, "Captive audience: exposed to the message frequently." To some, such blatant and unabashed ad creep is just one more example of unchecked consumerism. To date, Kroger, the number-one grocery-only chain in the country, has installed the belts in fifty-two Cincinnati locations as well as in stores across Arkansas, Mississippi, and Tennessee.[13]

Though they rarely attract much attention, the advertising industry is brimming with enterprising, insidious gimmicks like EnVision's Ads-N-Line. EggFusion uses lasers to inscribe ads on eggs. The China-based company 5Sai.com squeezes ads into the tiny spaces reserved by people's instant message names. Micro Target Media wraps portable toilets with advertising for Ford and Major League Baseball. Vision Media uses high-pressure water to etch ads into dirty sidewalks and walls. Beach'n Billboard creates drums for imprinting advertisements in sand. Ads are now played on American school buses, while the paper liners used on examination tables in doctors' offices often host advertisements.

Some makers of creeping ads, like Beach'n Billboard, which works in tandem with beach-cleaning machines, suggest that they're actually doing a public service as they vie for our attention. Such is the case with Freeload Press, a publishing company that's opening the doors for obsessive brands to extend their marketing into college textbooks.

"Liberating the textbook" since 2004, Freeload Press has been offering college students free digital textbooks (e-textbooks). The catch is a subtle slew of ads interspersed between algebra formulas and the principles of accounting 101, pitching brands like FedEx, Pura Vida Coffee, and Culvers, the Midwest restaurant chain famous for its frozen custard and "butterburgers." With increasingly expensive textbooks (the cost has tripled in the last twenty years according to the Government Accountability Office), the average student spends about $900 a year on books alone, fueling a $6.5 billion business.[14] More than one hundred U.S. colleges and universities now use Freeload's books. If a few ads can take the pressure off cash-strapped students, it's hard to argue with these colleges and universities for making the books available.

□   □   □

With so many easy and affordable ways to raise the profile of a company—from spam and online ads triggered by our own Web searches to hundreds of cable channels and falling print advertising rates—well-established brands are struggling to distinguish themselves in the crowd. Ironically, some are actually using shorter, cheaper ads to get attention. Aiming to deliver its message cheaper, faster, and innovatively, General Electric's "One-Second Theatre" is an example of one such "blink" (one-, two-, and five-second ads). GE stuffs thirty frames into a single second of

TV airtime, crossing its fingers that viewers will record the ads and play them back in slow motion. While these ads are uncommon compared to standard thirty-second spots, both Cadillac and AOL picked up five-second bits.[15]

The story is much the same on the radio, where, instead of "blinks," we hear "adlets." For one-fifth of the cost of a regular radio spot, Clear Channel, owner of 1,200 stations, sells five seconds of airtime. Two seconds cost just 10 percent of the standard rate—between $80 and $160. By stuffing ads into small breaks between songs, marketers hope to grab listeners' attention. (A two-second ad, after all, is almost unavoidable; it's over by the time you reach for the dial.)

The mania of obsessive branding disorder doesn't stop at the one-second barrier either. To raise their brands' profiles, companies have larded brand messages into slivers of a second—or blipverts. Appearing in emails, blipverts can flash words—like BUY! BUY!! BUY!!!—in multiple colors, in multiple sizes, and from multiple angles for as briefly as ten milliseconds. According to Richi Jennings, the eagle-eyed blogger who initially spotted the tiny pieces of spam, blipverts are designed to be small enough to slip by image-blocking spam filters unnoticed.

□   □   □

In an effort to make headway in a cluttered landscape, some major brands like Quicksilver, Mountain Dew, Ford, and Budweiser are effectively skipping the traditional advertisement process altogether to create their own films and shows. Known as branded entertainment, or advertainment, in most cases the medium allows brands complete control over how their products are featured. Early in 2007, in a move that aimed to expand its reign from the King of Beers to the king of branded media, Budweiser launched its multichannel network, BudTV, boasting exclusive video shorts from A-list stars like Matt Damon and Vince Vaughn, and BudTube, a "channel" that allows users to share homemade video clips, à la YouTube. (The format was essentially a bust: BudTV made little news after its launch, and traffic to the site is reported to have dropped off dramatically.)

While still a nascent movement, advertainment has nonetheless attracted a number of unlikely newcomers. Office Max created a product-littered sitcom, *Schooled*, for ABC Family; Snickers developed an online show about hip-hop stars turned superheroes; and megapublisher Harper-Collins (recently rebranded itself) struck a cozy deal with Fox's *Stacked*, the short-lived television series that featured a baffled Pamela Anderson wandering around a bookstore. (The books and promotional materials lining the walls of the fictional store were all supplied by HarperCollins.) Even Brawny, the paper towel brand, tried its hand at some branded content. Brawny Academy, a competitive online reality show, encouraged women to log on and "watch real husbands like yours learn from the Brawny Man himself."

Though some of the more mainstream examples of branded entertainment have found traction with audiences, consumers haven't warmed to the majority of brands' efforts.

□   □   □

Every day each of us contributes to the flush of commercial advertising with subtle nods to brands through the clothing we wear, the cars we drive, the coffee we drink. But most of us write off our purchasing decisions as the inevitable by-products of an age of industry: we have to clothe ourselves, and if we're lucky, we can afford to clothe ourselves in brands we like. And so we drape ourselves in a company product, we drive in branded vehicles, we sip grande lattes from the comfort of cushy couches in Starbucks. But our literal, physical bodies have traditionally remained apart from advertising. Clothed in product though they may be, our bodies have retained some sense of sacred space. In the current explosion of advertising, even this taboo seems to have gone by the wayside. Ad space on body parts is regularly auctioned off to the highest bidder. Babies are particularly hot properties. One St. Louis woman auctioned off the rights to sponsor the birth of her child and allowed a tech company to film the birth and post the event online. Her take for wearing company T-shirts and temporarily tattooing her pregnant belly with the company name was $1,000.[16] In 2005 a mother in North Carolina offered to sell ad space on her fifteen-month-old son; she offered a year's worth of advertising for $100,000, with smaller increments of time on offer through her website, www.buyjake.com.[17] At the same time, a Connecticut mother named her child GoldenPalace.com in exchange for $15,100 from the eponymous online casino.[18] (GoldenPalace.com also paid $10,000 for a permanent GoldenPalace.com tattoo on a Utah woman's forehead.[19])*

For people willing to put up some advertising at the altar, some companies, 1800FLOWERS and Smirnoff among them, have offered wedding sponsorship. With ads on the altar, it was only a matter of time before the sermomercial—the integration of commercial messages into religious sermons—would appear. Chrysler has reached out to African American churchgoers with a gospel tour through fourteen American megachurches. In 2006 Disney gave pastors everywhere the opportunity to win $1,000 and a trip to

---

*The market for branded animals has also exploded since 2005. In August 2005, the infamous GoldenPalace.com painted one hundred cows in Florida for use as billboards, and in 2006 several dogs in Germany were painted to promote a radio station. In September 2007, U.S.-based Conservation International auctioned off the rights to name ten new species of sharks discovered in Indonesia. Dinosaurs, insects, frogs, flowers—examples of all can be named for the right price. In fact, some brand names have become so interwoven into the fabric of our culture that they find their way into animal taxonomies without paying at all. The *Electrolux addisoni*, a South African ray, was christened in late 2007. An electric ray, it was named by the scientist who discovered it for the "vigorous sucking action" it displayed on the ocean floor.

Europe if they mentioned *The Chronicles of Narnia* from the pulpit.[20]

Clearly our obsession with branding has gone too far when priests are peddling Disney, liquor brands are sponsoring weddings, and mothers are selling the rights to name their children. Such extremes are sobering indications that ad creep and product placement have so polluted our cultural landscape that they've warped fundamental social and cultural institutions.

Above all else, the intent of branding is to sell. If it reshapes society subtly in the process, so much the better for the brand responsible. But the effect of so much branding has been a steady erosion in the public's trust. With each new branding ploy, consumers grow increasingly skeptical. In turn, companies are proving ever more willing to resort to deception and fake advertising to sell products. Such extreme examples of brands bartering in exchange for representation in what were traditionally sacred spaces illustrate an unhealthy willingness to exploit any opportunity if the price is right.

FIVE

Poisoning the
Grapevine

> Every man takes care that his neighbor shall
> not cheat him. But a day comes when he
> begins to care that he does not cheat his
> neighbor. Then all goes well.
>
> **RALPH WALDO EMERSON**,
> *The Conduct of Life*, 1860

If you search for "David Manning" online, you'll likely find a number of people, among them a British ambassador, a Major League Baseball pitcher, and a movie critic. The first two are genuine. The last was a figment of the imagination of a pair of marketing executives.

The twists and turns of David Manning's brief career as a film critic are arguably more intriguing than any of the movies he favorably reviewed. Created out of thin air by Sony executives in the summer of 2000, Manning purported to work for the *Ridgefield Press*, a bona-fide weekly in Connecticut unaware of its bogus employee. Manning, as it happened, had a penchant for films distributed by Columbia Pictures, a subsidiary of Sony. Though his flesh-and-blood peers were underwhelmed by Kevin Bacon as the transparent villain in 2000's *Hollow Man*, Manning couldn't get enough. "One helluva scary ride!" he proclaimed in ads printed around the country. Similar accolades followed for *A Knight's Tale*, *Vertical Limit*, and *The Patriot*. Manning even loved Rob Schneider's stinker *The Animal*, which he deemed "another winner."

By the following summer, however, Manning's upbeat tenure was up. Unable to contact the critic, a reporter for *Newsweek* revealed Manning's fabricated identity in June.[1] As the media rushed in, it was revealed that Sony had also been faking its television ads, in which employees were cast as satisfied moviegoers. (Universal Pictures, 20th Century Fox, and Artisan Entertainment later admitted to doing more or less the same thing.) Moviegoers swiftly filed a class-action lawsuit accusing the company of the "intentional and systematic deception of consumers."

Though Sony agreed to pull the remaining ads featuring Manning reviews and suspended the employees responsible, it saved its most audacious move for last. After the studio paid $326,000 to the state of Connecticut for its mendacity, it refused to refund moviegoers—arguing in court that the false Manning ads constituted free speech. An L.A. judge rejected the defense, and in 2005 Sony settled the suit out of court for $1.5 million. The studio never admitted liability.[2]

Perhaps it's to be expected that a multibillion-dollar film studio would dissemble and manipulate to such an extent. But the ultimate cost was hardly worth Sony openly flaunting its contempt for its consumers. (The $1.5 million settlement amounted to about 1 percent of the opening weekend's ticket sales of *Spiderman 2*, the studio's 2005 summer hit.) But given the current power and sway of big brands, the fact that Sony was held accountable—and actually paid up for its subterfuge— seems almost novel.

□   □   □

As a fictionalized character, Manning was a perfect corporate mouthpiece—he promoted product with a patina of legitimacy, at zero cost. Marketers understand that the best product endorsements come in the form of unsolicited praise from objective sources and satisfied customers. Some companies have taken the initiative to mimic such satisfaction with marketing ploys that capitalize on our desire to believe information streams that seem to flow from sources other than unsentimental capitalism.

In most cases, guerrilla, viral, and buzz marketing campaigns are harmless and largely ineffective. While they might fool us into picking up the abandoned wallet (purposely distributed with Bible verses inside) or warning the guy getting ready to drive away about the Starbucks cup on the roof of his car (it's glued there), such stunts are more silly than sneaky. One could argue that this kind of advertising erodes our Good Samaritan nature, turning us into jaded cynics and skeptics wary of being duped or speaking up, but such transgressions are minor compared to how far some brands are willing to go to make an impression.

In pursuit of revenue, advertisers are finding other ways to slip past our defenses and meddle with our often still-malleable opinions. Like hackers identifying vulnerabilities in security code, some brands are effectively hijacking long-trusted portals to bypass our bullshit filters.

In 2004 Volvo announced a phenomenal incident in which, by pure coincidence, thirty-two families in a small Swedish village had all bought the same Volvo sedan on the same day. Incredible as it was, the documentary film *The Mystery of Dalarö* attracted tens of thousands of viewers around the world. It took weeks for the dust to clear, but the film documenting the phenomenon—directed by Spike Jonze (*Adaptation*, *Being John Malkovich*)—was ultimately revealed to be a fake—albeit a good one. According to Volvo's global director of advertising, the stunt had achieved the desired result—to stir up conversation. Volvo went so far as to construct dummy websites and plant a tactful red herring (a separate making-of-the-film-type video addressing skeptics' questions). According to company execs, debates about the video's veracity sparked "the longest thread of conversation on one of the largest chat sites in [the Netherlands]."[3]

Each more outrageous than the last, viral campaigns are often creative, funny, and well produced. It's increasingly difficult to know if what we're seeing is real or fake (which is just the kind of nagging uncertainty that brands are counting on to get people talking). In pursuit of such intrigue, some brands have resorted to bald-faced lies in their efforts to cultivate online buzz, spinning fiction into reality with fake blogs (a.k.a. "flogs") and "astroturf"—organizations and programs that appear to be "grassroots efforts" but are actually brand-sponsored campaigns.

In 2003 Dr. Pepper scandalized bloggers around the world when the details of its efforts to promote its "Raging Cow" milk brand emerged. The company had asked six teenage bloggers not to mention that they'd been approached, trained, and given free drinks and products by the company in return for pitching the piña colada– and berry-flavored milk. Online critics launched a boycott of the brand, which disappeared from shelves after a year.

In December 2006, Sony paid two video bloggers to pose as teenagers desperate for a PlayStation Portable gaming system.[4] Jeremy and Charlie posted amateur rap videos about the product on YouTube and offered visitors PSP T-shirt iron-ons. Curious visitors could even find MySpace profiles of the boys. Their site, www.alliwantforchristmas isapsp.com, registered to a St. Louis marketing company employed by Sony, was ultimately discovered.

In some cases, brands use flogs and astroturf to counteract bad PR. Naturally, these efforts are risky—the more attention they get, the more likely they are to be uncovered as frauds. Edelman, the $300 million PR firm responsible for protecting brands like GM and Microsoft from bad press, has been caught several times concocting bogus news in favor of embattled mega-retailer Wal-Mart.

In March 2006, the *New York Times* revealed that Edelman had been working hand in hand with right-wing bloggers, "feeding them exclusive nuggets of news, suggesting topics for postings and even inviting them to visit its corporate headquarters."[5] (The campaign was discovered when the bloggers posted word-for-word passages from the PR firm as their own.) But such revelations were mild compared to what was to come just months later.

In late 2006, *BusinessWeek* outed "Jim" and "Laura," a pair of bloggers traversing the country in an RV who parked each night in a different Wal-Mart and sang the praises of the company in their blog "Wal-Marting Across America."[6] The RV, gas, and other travel expenses, as well as the blog, were all paid for by Edelman, which subsequently apologized and admitted to engineering two other pro–Wal-Mart sites.

□   □   □

Though a handful of viral videos and flogs have captured significant interest, the vast majority hardly register with consumers. Humorous online viral commercials like Smirnoff's "Teapartay" and Folger's "Happy Morning" often go largely unnoticed. Online marketing is, in this respect, no different than any other advertising medium. (Even the most creative ad firms can't predict with much accuracy what will generate the elusive buzz they're after.) Rather than guess and pour ad dollars into the Internet ether, many major brands are devoting their resources to marketing their products through personal exchanges between customers.

Word-of-mouth (WOM) marketing is rapidly becoming big business in the United States and around the world, despite its sometimes questionable ethics. The Word-of-Mouth Marketing Association (WOMMA) estimates that two-thirds of all economic activity in the United States is influenced by its industry. WOMMA counts among its members such recognized brands as American Express, Best Buy, Coca-Cola, and Sony. According to PQ Media, spending on WOM marketing in 2007 was an estimated $1.4 billion. By 2011, WOM spending is expected to reach $3.7 billion.[7]

At one time or another, almost everyone has been approached by a friend or relative trying to sell something. Companies that engage in door-to-door direct sales, like Amway, Avon, Tupperware, and Herbalife, have long followed the word-of-mouth model with success, pitching products through personal connections in return for everything from free samples of moisturizer to shiny pink Cadillacs.

According to the Direct Selling Association (the leading industry trade group), worldwide revenues from direct sales topped $89 billion last year. By their count, nearly 14 million people in the United States—about 8 percent of the adult population—are employed in the direct sales industry. Sales have nearly doubled in the past decade. Diet pills, furniture, vacuum cleaners, encyclopedias, plants, lingerie, pet food—you name it and chances are you've got a neighbor who can get a product for you at a "discount." Eager to reach new customers, name-brand companies are encouraging their most loyal devotees to sell goods in the cozy setting of their living rooms.

In 2001, following the Tupperware conscript-your-customers model, the beauty products retailer The Body Shop launched The Body Shop At Home. Besides "the opportunity to work with a globally recognized brand," members have access to loads of free products and promotional kits and can host themed, prepackaged events for their neighbors (among them the "Pure Pamper Party" or the "Flawless Facial Party"). Similarly, Crayola, the century-old crayon-making subsidiary of Hallmark, started enlisting customers to knock on doors in 2004. The company's "Big Yellow Box" initiative "promotes togetherness" by encouraging moms to hold crayon-selling parties for "friends, neighbors, co-workers and more."

But no matter how many trusted brands take part in direct sales, the industry will always be saddled with a certain stigma for the simple fact that many people find buying stuff from friends somewhat awkward. Word-of-mouth marketing, however, represents a significant evolution in face-to-face salesmanship and a controversial new front in our obsessive branding disorder. Rather than sell products outright, WOM participants may just talk glowingly about the merits of the item in question. Rather than inviting you to a party in their home, they may sidle up to you at work, in the bar, or over dinner at your house. Rather than tell you what they're up to, they'll keep their motives to themselves.

For the past several years, Procter & Gamble has been building the two most advanced and comprehensive WOM programs in the world. Tremor, founded in 2000 to create and manage buzz in the teen market, now counts 250,000 teens among its members. Vocalpoint, Tremor's equivalent for mothers, has amassed some 600,000 advocates. Recruited through websites, banner ads, emails, and fellow members, these mothers and children aren't just hawking Procter & Gamble wares. For a fee, P&G hires their recruits out to brands in the entertainment, fashion, music, food, and beauty industries. At last count, 80 percent of Tremor's clients were non–Procter & Gamble brands—companies like Coca-Cola, ABC, Toyota, and the music label EMI. About 50 percent of Vocalpoint brand clients are external.

P&G emphasizes that the free products and samples in its programs are offered in exchange for participation, not as a form of compensation. Assuming that they like the products, members are encouraged to sing their praises to friends and family (and pass on a coupon or two).

Tremor and Vocalpoint have, from Procter & Gamble's standpoint, been a huge success. Though Procter & Gamble guards clients and results closely, according to early press reports, Vocalpoint delivered double-digit sales increases in test markets.[8]

If Procter & Gamble's numbers are right, one in every one hundred kids in the United States works for Tremor, and about seven in every one hundred U.S. moms works for Vocalpoint. Don't be surprised if you haven't heard of either program before. As with a number of other WOM efforts, neither Tremor nor Vocalpoint requires that its members reveal their affiliation.

The idea that a neighbor could be surreptitiously selling us a new type of deodorant or toothpaste in return for free goods is inherently repulsive. But like the bugs that lodge themselves in the corners of our television screens, word-of-mouth marketing has spread without much objection from mainstream media or society at large. The consensus seems to indicate instead that we ought to get used to it or tune it out. If 7 percent of the mothers in the United States are members of Vocalpoint, it's troubling to consider how nonmembers distinguish between a genuine Pampers recommendation and an incentivized pitch. Dissembling to promote diapers is not a concern for most of us, but if secretly promoting products to friends and neighbors in return for coupons and free goods is legal, it's imaginable that word-of-mouth could become increasingly commonplace.

Seventy-six percent of consumers cite word-of-mouth product recommendations as their primary sources of information for making purchasing decisions.[9] As these channels become more polluted with marketing, that number will fall. As it does, it will act like a social barometer, tracing the falling level of trust and goodwill in our culture. It's easy to imagine where this will lead: progressively more jaded consumers will become wary of the slightest hint of ulterior motives, real or not. Consumers will gradually come to view all but their closest friends as possible salespeople. Lacking the ability to trust each other, we will become increasingly isolated and lose a fundamental faculty for forming strong communities.

□   □   □

In 1922 U.S. Commerce Secretary Herbert Hoover announced in the first National Conference on Radio Telephony, "It is inconceivable that we should allow so great a possibility for service to be drowned in advertising chatter." The debate over whether or not to allow advertising on the radio was a heated national controversy that continued for years before broadcasters and listeners eventually acquiesced and advertisers were able to take advantage of the medium to peddle their wares.

Nearly a century later, advertising continues to raise hackles whenever it's introduced to a new medium, though consumers have shown an impressive willingness to put up with it. Never before has advertising advanced so quickly, however, into so many new areas of our lives, or been as difficult to discern. With the advent of covert WOM programs like Tremor and Vocalpoint, our friends and neighbors are potential extensions of brand identity.

Walter Carl, an assistant professor of communications at Northeastern University and an advisory board member with WOMMA, sees Procter & Gamble's WOM efforts as legal but unethical. For more than a decade, Carl diligently recorded, sequenced, and mapped countless kitchen-table chats, long-distance calls to Mom, and happenstance hallway huddles with coworkers in an effort to study how we communicate with each other. During the past several years, Carl has focused his research on marketing and on studying how corporate messages travel through conversation. It's his position that marketers should require customer advocates to disclose their connection to the brands they serve.

But even as branding infiltrates the most intimate circles of our private lives, neither our public laws nor our personal logic has kicked in to halt the invasion. Gary Ruskin, Commercial Alert's executive director, believes WOM marketing is fraudulent and a violation of law. In the fall of 2005, he sent his complaints to the Federal Trade Commission (FTC), requesting that the commission investigate WOM programs like those at Procter & Gamble and set specific guidelines for the industry at large. The complaint prompted a flood of sensational press lamenting what was ridiculed as transgressive marketing campaigns with frightening potential. Even mainstream business voices that typically championed Procter & Gamble's branding prowess, such as *Advertising Age* and *BusinessWeek*, spoke out against the nebulous ethics behind Vocalpoint and Tremor.[10]

In December 2006, following a year of research and deliberation, the FTC declined Ruskin's request, saying that it was not necessary to issue guidelines yet. But the commission did acknowledge some concerns about WOM marketing tactics. Responding to Ruskin's complaint, Mary Engle, the FTC's associate director for advertising practices, admitted that certain cases of WOM were potentially "deceptive," especially where marketers weren't required to disclose their affiliations to a company and product.[11]

Contacted by phone to discuss the decision, Engle emitted a long sigh before acknowledging that WOM marketing is part of an ongoing conversation at the FTC. "It's a hard question," she said. "We agreed with Gary. If companies are paying advocates, they need to disclose that."

The tricky part for regulators like Engle is that programs like Tremor and Vocalpoint offer free products and samples rather than cash in exchange for buzz. According to the FTC's "Endorsement and Testimonial Guides," "When there exists a connection between the endorser and the seller of the advertised product which might materially affect the weight or credibility of the endorsement . . . such connection must be fully disclosed."

The bottom line is that the FTC cares only if consumers care. If consumers feel that brands shouldn't be allowed to supply certain customers with free goods and services in return for promotional work, then the FTC will listen. According to Engle, consumers aren't raising too much of a fuss about WOM.

But what if the "product sample" is a free laptop, a cell phone, or something of significant material value? About this, Engle is less sure. From her response ("drawing the line is important") it seems clear that we're in the early days of a largely unregulated industry—one that captures us in unanticipated ways, perhaps especially when it crosses the line between an obvious sale and a friend's casual endorsement of a product worth paying attention to.

Ultimately, the free stuff may not be as much of an issue as critics believe. After observing WOM programs for over a year, Engle says that the real appeal to many participants in advocate programs isn't the free gear but the feeling of community and the opportunity to play a role in a multimillion-dollar marketing campaign.

□   □   □

According to researchers at the University of California at Berkeley and the Massachusetts Institute of Technology, the positive feelings we experience from participating when others ask us to help accomplish tasks or solve problems may be more influential than money or gifts. In the 2004 study "Effort for Payment: A Tale of Two Markets," published in the journal *Psychological Science*, researchers James Heyman and Dan Ariely set out to "shed light on the well-established observation that people sometimes expend more effort in exchange for no payment . . . than they expend when they receive low payment."[12]

To explore the idea, Heyman and Ariely* conducted a series of experiments in which they offered subjects different types of rewards in exchange for help. In one, they asked people how willing they might be to help load a sofa into a van. In return, some participants were offered varying amounts of money, some were offered candy bars and boxes of chocolate, and some were offered nothing in return for their labor. Predictably, the more money Heyman and Ariely offered the first group, the more willing they were to help. In the second group, regardless of how much candy was offered, subjects' willingness to help remained largely the same. Those who were offered no reward

---

*Ariely, now the Alfred P. Sloan Professor of Business Economics at the MIT Sloan School of Management, expanded upon his research in a February 2008 book, *Predictability Irrational: The Hidden Forces that Shape Our Decisions.*

were more willing to help than those compensated with candy or small amounts of money.

Simply introducing the idea of money changed people's attitudes toward the work they were asked to do. After revealing the monetary value of the candy being offered to the second group of participants, the researchers found that subjects' willingness to help actually dropped. They reached similar findings in two further experiments—including one in which the subjects' efforts were measured by the amount of time they spent trying to solve a numbers puzzle (which actually had no solution). In this last experiment, people who weren't offered anything worked longer than those offered money or candy. Without a tangible reward, participants considered their contributions in terms of goodwill.

When payment is introduced as an incentive, people's interest in lending a hand is complicated by their scrutiny of the suggested compensation. Consider applying the same logic to your car. If an automaker offered you $50 to promote your new car at work and among your friends and family for a month, the very offer of money begs the question, why not $100? Why not $500? Isn't access to my network worth at least that much? Brands have discovered that by simply offering some sense of *involvement* in a brand community, they can entice consumers to act as commercials.

□   □   □

"We are the ones who watch the shows, and buy the products, and spread the lotions, and eat the foods, and take the medicines, and clean the dirt, and wear the clothes, and influence our communities. . . . For all of you Vocalpoint Member-Moms out there, keep up the good work! Thank you, Vocalpoint, for a really, great time!"

The enthusiastic words belong to "Barbara," a Vocalpoint member and a self-proclaimed forty-five-year-old suburban mother with three boys. Written as part of a thank-you note for Vocalpoint's invitation to a media-related press event in New York, her letter appeared on Vocalpoint's website, complete with photos of Barbara alongside fellow guests Carmen Electra and former Miss USA Tara Conner.

For all the free coupons, samples, and products Tremor and Vocalpoint provide their members, the primary motivator for participation is arguably the intangible sense of "belonging." As with Cova's "brand tribes," P&G's hundreds of thousands of marketing recruits derive a sense of community and value from their role as "consumer advocates." Vocalpoint's tagline is "Be heard." Tremor's website offers the same promise.

Following the FTC's decision not to set guidelines for the industry, Gary Ruskin of Commercial Alert believes that the larger social ramifications of WOM marketing are a legitimate and pressing concern. Ruskin admits, "It's something the law can't take into account. This is the sad part. With the spread of word-of-mouth marketing, we have less reason to trust our friends and family. Parents should be aware—it's conceivable that our kids are deceiving us for profit."

In case studies in which people were unaware that they were being marketed to, a 5 percent "negative backlash effect" was observable when the subject discovered the truth.[13] In such cases, the negative impression extended to the advocate, the brand, and sometimes the company that made the brand. As its name suggests, word-of-mouth marketing can work both ways—when a product gets a bad rap, this type of under-the-radar tactic can hurt.

With the continual spread of WOM, it's possible to imagine a future in which consumers will demand that the lines between commercial and community be more clearly drawn. If federal laws are not passed that would temper the spread of WOM, it's likely that business will reach a point where particular trusted organizations offer validations or seals verifying "a WOM-free home" or "a WOM-free business." As much as the average Vocalpoint mom may enjoy the sense of community provided by Procter & Gamble, as well as the free products, samples, and perks, if the majority of mothers are sponsored by brands, it stretches the boundaries of commerciality. There's little reason to believe the WOM trend will stop at shampoo or dish soap. The cost of not being able to take anyone's words at face value is a hollow social environment, one that, unsurprisingly, might make us more skeptical of one another's motivations at every turn.

Although it might seem that branding could not encroach *any* further into our personal lives, advances in science and technology have inspired exploration into the yet more intimate field of sensory branding. By sculpting the invisible olfactory and aural branding channels around us, branding initiatives are offering up fascinating feedback on how our senses process information. But consumers won't benefit from the insights of this sensory revolution. On the contrary, consumers will need to adapt to a new form of branding in their lives. Progressively cornered by ad creep, and more skeptical by the day, we must prepare ourselves for a new era of multisensory, often invisible, branding.

Invisible
Branding

> Seeing that the senses cannot decide our
> dispute, being themselves full of uncertainty,
> we must have recourse to reason.
>
> MICHEL DE MONTAIGNE (1533–92),
> *The Essays of Montaigne*

Beginning in 1938, a curious new safety feature began appearing on cars in Buick Motor Company showrooms around the United States. Electronic turn signals, or "trafficators," as some manufacturers described them, had been available for years as a specialty after-market product and on some luxury foreign cars, but before Buick, no major U.S. auto manufacturer saw any reason to offer them as standard equipment.[1]

For the first thirty years of the automobile, drivers communicated by waving at each other. To indicate that he was turning, a driver had to remove his hand from the wheel, reach out the window, and signal with his arm. With the introduction of electronic turn signals, drivers could simply flip a switch or press a button near the steering wheel and a blinking light would indicate their intended direction.

Initially an optional accessory, blinkers soon became mandatory. Since 1938, bulbs have been added to the chassis and wattages have changed, but little in the indicator has evolved as far as the mechanics are concerned: the driver depresses a lever, an innocuous tapping indicates the signal, and a light flashes outside the car.

And for seventy years, automakers have essentially ignored the sound of the blinker. Whether you bought a Dodge Wayfarer in 1950, a Ford Falcon in 1974, or a gleaming $70,000 Chevrolet Corvette ZR–1 in 1995, one turn signal sounded pretty much just like any other.

In 2008 drivers and their passengers will spend an average of eighteen hours listening to blinkers.[2] According to branding guru Martin Lindstrom, we have overlooked the blinker for far too long.

If the engineers at Ford or Toyota take the time to design and install a turn indicator (or pay one of their subsidiaries to do so), why should it be generic? Automobile brand names are already carefully positioned all over the finished product, from the steel of the grill to the fabric of the seats. Why hasn't it occurred to anyone to make the blinker in a Ford sound different from the one in a Chevy? It certainly hasn't been a regulatory issue. Current law requires that turn signals flash at a standardized rate—between 60 and 120 times a minute—but says nothing about the sound they make. For all the law cares, blinkers could emit a steady one-note tone or play a five-act operatic opus. But the sound of blinkers has stayed the same. Until now.

Someday you'll be able to close your eyes behind the wheel and distinguish the make of a vehicle simply by the sound of the turn signal. This is but one of many anticipated sensory branding channels to command our attention in years to come. Standing in line at a fast-food restaurant a few years from now, customers might be able to recognize where they are just by the sound that straws make as fellow patrons poke them through the lids of their drinks. Today we can get a whiff of sensory branding just by walking down some grocery store aisles where we can smell a light fragrance emanating from plastic coupon dispensers.

Increasingly, corporations are relying on sensory branding to occupy our attention spans in an effort to co-opt our consciousness. In this way, brands are lobbying for unclaimed spaces in the world around us. Close your eyes and you'll still smell the brand. Plug your nose and you'll still hear it. A British branding firm recently started developing undisclosed subtle scents to include inside packs of Pall Mall and Lucky Strike cigarettes. Korean tire manufacturer KUMHO began introducing lavender-, jasmine-, and orange-scented tires in 2007. In the United

States, marketers are using "audiobeam" technology to allow grocery and bookstore ads to "whisper" to one customer at a time. As is the nature of cutting-edge branding, the goal with sensory initiatives is to tap into a customer's emotional side.

◻   ◻   ◻

Martin Lindstrom, the guru who would brand the blinker and the founder of the sensory branding consultancy Brandsense, was born in Holland. At thirty-eight, his impish smile and convivial personality are complemented by a fierce intelligence and boundless energy. Lindstrom has been involved in branding for most of his life. At the age of twelve, he was hired by Lego as a consultant after the company discovered he'd been attracting tourists and making local news by building model cities out of its product. Today he dedicates himself to consulting with prominent corporations, looking for ways to seduce our subconscious with sensory appeals.

Effectively, Lindstrom has built a career and a consulting agency out of helping corporations reach deep into the experience of the average consumer and stake claims on the sights, sounds, smells, tastes, and tactile experiences associated with their products and services. At Brandsense, specialists research and brainstorm the overlooked, unclaimed spaces in our lives. Lindstrom's staff is scattered across the globe, and Lindstrom, the czar of sensory branding, is a fount of unanticipated trivia: Kellogg's honed the distinctive crunchiness of its cornflakes in a Dutch sound lab; Singapore Airlines has a branded scent, music, and fabric. Eighty-three percent of all advertising appeals to our eyes only. Seventy-five percent of our everyday emotions are influenced by our sense of smell. "There's a sixty-five percent chance of a mood change when exposed to a positive sound."* Whether we believe him or not, companies are increasingly paying attention to the ways in which we are inspired to make purchases. "Ninety-five percent of what we do is unconscious," according to Lindstrom. "With sensory branding, we are opening a Pandora's box that will reshape the world."

If Lindstrom's estimate is correct, 89 billion times a year the awkward hoot of the fast-food straw announces itself. With that in mind, it's hard to argue with his conviction that the straw is a much-overlooked branding opportunity. If he's right, we are programmed to get thirsty at the sound of a straw—a sound indicative of fast food.

□   □   □

No less impressive than our sense of hearing, the human nose can recognize over ten thousand aromas. Plastic has never been a favorite. Adam Bell saw that as a challenge to

---

*Lindstrom's numbers are from a Millward Brown study of the five senses in which six hundred researchers worked across more than a dozen countries.

overcome. Bell is a plastics guy, the CEO of Rotuba Extrusions, a fifty-eight-year-old New Jersey company. For years Rotuba has been making high-impact, durable plastics, like those used to make Sears Craftsman tools. But Rotuba is also the creator of a lesser-known product called Auracell, a dynamic plastic material that can take on any shape and any smell.

Years ago Bell presented air freshener manufacturers with red plastic that smelled like a flower, but they turned him down. The sensory tide has since turned, and Bell has seen a sharp increase in orders for Auracell. Many major brands (Tide among them) get their perfumes from Bell's 33,000-scent library. Others, like toy and cell-phone manufacturers, are just entering the market.

In 2005 New America Marketing (a division of News Corp) began installing fruit punch–scented coupon dispensers in the aisles of Shaw's and Acme grocery stores to promote children's Motrin. Engineered to be smelled from three to four inches away, the dispensers drew curious customers near (particularly children, whose noses passed closer to them) without assaulting their senses.

In 2005 Home Depot began selling Auracell-based scent clips for air purifiers. Customers at New York's trendy Scoop stores can now choose from eight different Auracell-scented bangles, sampling from mimosa, black currant, and honeysuckle. By 2006, Auracell had found its way into cell phones, with models like the high-end LG "white chocolate" slider. (Contrary to the name, the keypad is infused with a lavender scent.) Bell has also been approached by liquor companies interested in using Auracell on their bottles as a subtle reminder of their product's fragrance. Most recently, Auracell was introduced to a line of cosmetic brushes.

With dozens of Auracell products currently in the works, from cologne-infused golf tees to toys and mobile phones, Rotuba's sales doubled in 2007. Kimberly-Clark has been working with Bell to infuse Huggies diapers with scented material, and Unilever is investigating scented plastic for its Suave shampoo bottles. One major video rental chain is looking into actually building into its stores the scent of buttered popcorn.

Aside from the far-reaching campaigns striving to attract our olfactory senses, the most interested players on the sensory frontier have been the perfume companies themselves. While Auracell plastic is about three times as expensive as paper, major perfume manufacturers will be rolling out plastic testers in the near future. Presented with a sample that retains its scent, people are less likely to discard it. The same holds true for a hair clip or a pair of J-Lo sunglasses.

If a consumer can figure out what a product smells like from the cellophane wrap or the lid of a package, there's no need to open the box or break any seals. And scents present an opportunity to verify brand authenticity and to distinguish the genuine article from the knockoff. If it doesn't have that trademark odor, it's not the real deal.

Even brands without a necessarily marketable scent are engaging in olfactory marketing. Embracing the concept of the "sensory stay," major hotel chains now pump perfume into their lobbies, be it lavender or sage, lemongrass or green tea. For soccer's 2006 World Cup in Germany, a local company erected "smelling posts" for each nation represented. (France smelled of Chanel No. 5, England of After Eight mints, and the United States of Coca-Cola.)

Public transit is also getting smelly. To get people thinking about milk, the California Milk Processor Board began infusing San Francisco bus stops with the scent of freshly baked cookies. In Union Square, Nob Hill, or the Financial District, passengers can get a whiff of Grandma's kitchen. Lest commuters crave cookies rather than milk, the campaign's message is driven home with "Got Milk?" ads, which have been prominently featured at bus stops.[3]

With olfactory branding, companies are counting on scent to create an emotional shortcut to our purchasing decisions. While most perfumes aren't targeted at an actual "experience," a number of smells have proven effects on our moods, our metabolic rate, and our alertness. Melon has been shown to inspire friendliness, and musk to shorten women's menstrual cycles, increase ovulation, and improve the chances of conception. If shrewdly determined, the right scent can provide marketers with access to the inner workings of our biology and our subconscious. Notably, artificial fragrances are not subject to government regulation.

In case study after case study, Lindstrom points to scenarios in which scent has been shown to influence consumer behavior and to increase sales. Consumers in one Brandsense study preferred a pair of Nikes showcased in a scented room 84 percent more than an identical pair in an unscented room. (They were even prepared to pay $10.23 more for the scented pair.) The casino brand Harrah's Entertainment discovered that pumping pleasant smells into gambling areas boosted slot machine revenues by 45 percent.

□　□　□

Food is a long-standing example of sensory branding. To the person who indulges in one fast-food meal a year, the difference between a Big Mac and a Whopper is negligible. But to the fastidious consumer, there's a discernible difference. Only during the late twentieth century, in an attempt to extend their brands into the larger realm of customer experience, did large numbers of traditionally non-food-related brands begin defining themselves through taste.

Encouraging fans to "taste the excitement," NASCAR recently launched an entire line of branded meats in grocery stores around the country, including hot dogs, bacon, and sausage.[4] Licensed grilling and sandwich meats are, in essence, a statement to consumers about the "NASCAR lifestyle." (While many brands would stop there, NASCAR has tapped into lifestyle extensions—from laptops to chainsaws to romance novels—for more than $2 billion in revenue a year.)[5] Crayon manufacturer Crayola has also found its way into the grocery aisle with Crayola Color Coolerz, a line of children's beverages made with elementary-school lunch boxes in mind.

Companies eager to leverage taste in the name of the brand can now hire any number of firms. Nomad, a French food-branding and design company that works to link brands to culinary experiences, "develops original recipes inspired by a concept, identity or product . . . to echo an organization's values and effectively communicate a brand message." While a typical caterer may provide a company with set menu items for a product launch or company event, Nomad creates a custom menu inspired by the client.

For a Heineken event, Nomad catered finger foods that went well with beer. In an effort to mimic Heineken's green-and-white bottle, Nomad presented white finger foods on a green grass motif. In contrast, an event for Bloomberg Financial featured stark, futuristic food with a more international flare, like vertical strands of gourmet ice cream extending from tiny cones. Unlike the loose and informal look and feel of the Heineken event, plates and cups at the Bloomberg fete were aligned with an eye for order and symmetry. With the goal of forming branding associations that will endure, sensory branders know that texture and shape play a key role in taste-marketing venues. While high-end caterers have always been known for their lavish spreads, Nomad's approach to food has piqued the curiosity of a number of high-profile clients interested in seeing their brands imaginatively translated for the palate.

□   □   □

Establishing aural associations with products through often woefully unforgettable jingles is perhaps the oldest form of sensory branding. But in a more technically advanced world, this age-old advertising medium is now provoking us through often unanticipated formats. One such example is the use of high-tech sonic equipment in retail spaces.

"Hey, you, over here. Don't turn around," a nearby voice whispers as you walk through the mystery section of your bookstore. You turn, but no one is there. "Can you hear me? Do you ever think about murder, committing the ultimate crime? I do. All the time."

The conspiratorial voice isn't that of a sociopath. It's a high-tech acoustic device dubbed the "mystery whisperer." Installed in the aisles of a handful of Manhattan bookstores by Court TV to promote a series of murder mysteries called "Murder by the Book," the targeted device delivers sound waves with a concentrated "audiobeam" activated by a motion sensor.[6] Standing in the Stephen King section, you hear it. Sidle on over to the Jonathan Kellerman thrillers, a foot to the left, and you don't.

Known as directional sound, audiobeams project sound waves in much the same way as a spotlight projects light. The resulting sound is disquieting—the listener actually feels as if the noise is coming from an invisible pair of headphones, or from inside his head. Capable of projecting hundreds of feet and bouncing off flat surfaces, like a wall or a TV screen, audiobeams are ideal for delivering messages in public spaces already overcrowded with noise. (Early adopters of the technology have included Disney's Epcot Center and museums like the Smithsonian National Air and Space Museum and the Boston Museum of Science.)

From SWAT teams to the Navy to auto manufacturers, directional sound has countless applications, but it is perhaps the most promising as an advertising tool. In 2006 In-Store Broadcasting Network, "the largest retail place–based media company in the world" (servicing chains like Kroger, Safeway, Walgreen's, and Duane Read), began installing twelve thousand audiobeam devices in supermarket and drugstore aisles. If you haven't heard one yet, you will soon.

Increasingly, big brands are spending big bucks on sonic branding. Beyond traditional jingles and "audio logos," the desire to keep every note "on brand" now extends to company conference music, internal training software, and the Muzak that customers hear while they are on hold. Conformity and uniformity are key. The driving force behind branding the sensory landscape is to own and control every last moment shared between the customer and the brand. Such work can't be left to just any rank-and-file employee. Today sonic branding is handed over to the specialists—and highly paid composers and sound engineers are playing a tune that executives just can't ignore.

□   □   □

It's 3:00 PM in Manhattan, and though the honking, roaring crush of taxis and commuters isn't due for another two hours, it's rush hour at the Best Buy in Chelsea. "Three o'clock is the witching hour," says Audrey Arbeeny, a sonic branding specialist and trained flutist with a conspiratorial flash of mischief. "There are a couple of high schools nearby. The kids get out for the day and come to hang out." Dressed uniformly in oversized T-shirts and low-slung backpacks, small tribes of fifteen-year-olds, mostly boys, meander through the aisles, shuffling through racks of Ludacris and Christina Aguilera CDs and posing for goofy pictures with the store's digital cameras—tethered floor models already showing signs of wear from the daily flood of curious teenagers.

Arbeeny goes to Best Buy to linger by the display for the Xbox 360, Microsoft's popular video game console. On a typical afternoon, teenage boys stand in a semicircle, joking with each other as they wrestle with the game's controls, the rapid clicking of tiny buttons providing a spastic backbeat to the sound effects pouring from the speakers. Unable to contain herself, Arbeeny gestures to the screen and announces that she is responsible for creating the game's sounds. The boys pause, turning to size up the middle-aged stranger with the Staten Island accent, her blond bangs framing a what-do-you-think-of-that kind of smile. "Yeah," they say. "Right."

Arbeeny is the cofounder and executive director of Audiobrain, one of the premier sonic branding firms in the world. The sounds she's boasting about aren't the chattering of machine guns or the screeching of tires. In fact, it's unlikely that any of the boys in Best Buy have ever consciously noticed the sounds Arbeeny is known for, though they've probably heard them more than any other sound in any other game. The humdrum, everyday sound that buttons in the main menu make when pressed are repeated billions of times every day. At first acoustically invisible, they're ubiquitous in the Xbox 360; contributing a small handful of branded sounds that players hear regardless of the game being played. Whether you're shooting Russian infantrymen in "Call of Duty," plowing line drives in "MVP Baseball," or vaporizing aliens in a galaxy far, far away in "Star Wars Battlefront," the sounds you hear in the Xbox menu are Audiobrain's.

Audiobrain's staff, almost all of whom are graduates of the prestigious Berklee College of Music, features five trained composers. American Express, IBM, and HBO are among the global corporations that rely on Audiobrain for sonic branding, from audio logos and ring tones to mood-setting pieces played in the background during sales conferences and on-hold music for customer hotlines. Located in Manhattan's Flatiron District, the company's offices are tucked behind an unmarked door in a nondescript building. Throughout the office, noisy air conditioners hum, rattle, and buzz. At the heart of the office is a recording studio, an oasis of silence sealed away from the rest of the rooms. Sound equipment is stacked halfway up the walls. On the day I visited the staff had been up until three in the morning working on an NFL commercial.

Dr. Seuss's Thing 1 and Thing 2 hang from either side of an aging Mac screen in Arbeeny's otherwise austere office. "Companies look to us because they know what they want it to look like but they don't understand how to translate the personality of the company into sound," Arbeeny explains. "Most people would be incredibly surprised that the little sound they hear—*bleep*—could take so much effort by so many people to create."

In the case of the Xbox menu noise, which is more of a *swoosh* than a *bleep*, Audiobrain spent countless hours developing the right tone and pitch, going through a vast catalog of sounds, from the rattle and clatter of falling sheet metal to a saw biting through various materials to the slicing ring of a just-brandished sword. Arbeeny and her staff tested their arsenal of eclectic instruments in the studio, one by one, recording each *twang*, *rattle*, and *whoosh* in the search for just the right feel. The result was an auditory cue somewhere in the neighborhood of a breathy *phoo*. Like the blinker, the sound is deeply rooted in the experience of the brand. After hearing it over and over, players will eventually ignore it. But hearing it out of context, on TV or online, they will be suddenly snapped back to the game and the brand.

The Pavlovian noises of the Xbox video game system are highly desirable to businesses looking for any means of snagging consumers' attention. Investment funds, health care conglomerates, and any number of other major industries have recently embraced similar audio branding techniques. Southwest Airlines has made particularly clever use of its trademark one-note *Ding!*—the same unmistakable noise heard on any airline when the FASTEN SEAT BELT light comes on—in TV commercials and on the Web. Customers can even install the company's *Ding!* software on their computer's desktop—so as to hear the familiar sound throughout the day whenever Southwest posts a new low fare.

Arbeeny is proud of her work, but she is clearly most taken by the Xbox 360's official audio logo—a sound heard on video game advertisements and the first sound gamers hear when they turn on their systems. In creating the audio logo, Audiobrain considered its psychological and philosophical requirements. "We knew we had to make the sound sustainable and complex," says Arbeeny. "It had to be social and inclusive, organic, multidimensional, full of energy."

Audiobrain started with the product's name, Xbox 360. After testing various individual voices with the five syllables, engineers tried the sound of many different overlapping voices. Not quite satisfied, they repeated the same experiment with multiple voices speaking in six different languages. Bingo. Turn on an Xbox 360 today and the first noise you hear—that brief slipstream of airy voices—is the result. Everything after that was fine-tuning.

In the earlier years of the company, Audiobrain might have settled there, grateful for the opportunity to design sounds inside a game console that has sold some 12 million units to date. But today sonic branding demands a bigger slice of the branding pie. From the custom-crafted sounds of car doors slamming to the classic *potato-potato* report of a Harley-Davidson engine, executives are listening when the sonic gurus come calling.

After selling Microsoft on their final sound, the Audiobrain team suggested steps the company could take to beef up the console's sonic branding in other areas, such as at events, in advertising, and in online media. Soon, not only was Audiobrain invited to help select the band at the company's next Xbox 360 event, but Audiobrain was managing sonic branding across multiple Microsoft media channels. Prior to spending an estimated $100 million on the launch of the Zune,[7] the MP3 player many thought would be an "iPod killer," Microsoft tapped Audiobrain for all the gizmo's "product sonification."

Arbeeny admits that the subtleties she and her staff obsessed over for the Xbox audio logo are almost impossible to hear. But obsession is the price companies are willing to pay to distinguish themselves. For a large project like NBC's Sydney Olympics, Audiobrain created seven thousand pieces of branded sound—from split-second crackles played between score charts to grand operatic pieces during broadcasts of major events.

Audiobrain projects often start out with a "sound audit," a process during which Arbeeny and her colleagues listen to every sound associated with a brand— from corporate videos to on-hold music to advertising voice-overs and jingles. Even internal human resource tapes and conference music get a listen. Often, clients have no idea what they're in for. During one sound audit of a major company, Arbeeny's call to the company's main office number was answered by what sounded to her like "a seventy-five-year-old chain-smoker." Recalling the experience, she clenches her fists. "This is a company with very sexy voices in its ads. Way off brand! They'll spend millions on advertising and this chain-smoking old lady answers the phone?" Overlooking such aspects of a customer's experience can offer mixed messages about a brand. Good branding seeks to create an image that is consistently uniform, and like LPK's "Tool Box Vision," Audiobrain offers a "sonic branding toolbox," sold as part of a "complete palette of emotional and experiential sound crafted through the brand's unique sonic lens."

Despite their fees (they make between $50,000 and $1 million per project), Audiobrain is in high demand with some of the biggest brands in the world. Ninety-eight percent of Arbeeny's clients return for further work, and in the past year revenues have doubled and four different companies have offered to buy out her company. Executives are only just beginning to tune in to the idea of spending a million bucks for a few seconds of branding sound. IBM is one Audiobrain client that can't seem to get enough.

□　□　□

Arbeeny has been creating audio branding for IBM since 1998. Whether you're visiting IBM's website, calling the company's help line, or attending an IBM conference, chances are the sounds you'll hear were designed and approved by Audiobrain. Even IBM's internal training programs feature Audiobrain sounds. One of Arbeeny's favorite stories is of a sound audit she did for IBM's Linux group years ago. "They put me on hold and I had silence," she says. "And then the silence changed to a different silence, a white-noise silence." This is just the kind of thing that gets under a sonic branding specialist's skin (and flies right over everyone else's head)—two clashing types of silence.

After going to an IBM conference in 2001, Arbeeny sent the event coordinator a memo in which she offered an overview of what she saw as a cacophony of arbitrary music choices that had little in common with the conference in question. Considering her complaint, IBM teamed up with Audiobrain to create a fourteen-track "IBM Event Music Album" that "incorporate[s] many of the brand's attributes . . . in order to create an experience that sonically supports the IBM brand." Highlights include music tracks for various moments of any given corporate conference, such as a "Keynote Speaker Walk-on," "Break Music," and a "Hyped Walk-on" (intended to create a rallying spirit).

Like it or not, today's consumers are already the guinea pigs of a corporate sensory branding renaissance. If companies brand with smells and sounds the same way they do with billboards and spam, issues like sensory pollution and sensory manipulation are a foregone conclusion. Underlying these visceral concerns is the troublingly obsessive element of extended branding. At first glance (or scent, or sound), sensory innovations are intriguing, but such innovation assumes a different cast after companies have mined our environment for years for branding possibilities. Looking ahead, it's possible to imagine a time when an everyday assault of commercial brand-ordained smells, textures, colors, and sounds will be ever more imposing and bureaucratically inspired.

Getting Inside Our
Heads

In the beginning was the secret brain.
The brain was celled and soldered in the thought.

DYLAN THOMAS, "In the Beginning"

By the summer of 2004, Mart Martin had bounced around Atlanta with Coca-Cola for over ten years, and he had seen countless promotional campaigns come and go. But he'd never seen a launch like C2, Coke's low-carb cola. It had it all: a $50 million marketing budget with rock music licensed from the Rolling Stones and Queen, a debut during the *American Idol* finals, and NASCAR drivers in bright-red C2 fire suits, ripping around the nation in C2 race cars. To top it off, Atkins and South Beach, two blockbuster diets, were introducing more consumers to the low-carb craze every day, a trend that promised to propel the mid-calorie "Real

Thing" scion to the top right corner of the sales charts. Market research at Pepsi reported that 60 million potential customers were standing by for a mid-calorie solution. This was the big one.

Martin didn't hold back in the press. C2 was Coca-Cola's largest product launch since Diet Coke—one that would require significant company manpower and resources. In an effort to steal the spotlight, Pepsi had rushed its mid-calorie Edge onto the market two months ahead of schedule. Coke was coming out, guns blazing.

As the proud executives in Atlanta, Georgia, and Purchase, New York, lined up to christen their gleaming new offerings in an explosion of mid-calorie froth, consumers took one sip, shrugged, and walked away. Month after agonizing month, the meager sales figures came in. The estimates of a vast, untapped market of 60 million mid-calorie customers were apparently grossly overblown. According to October's *Beverage Digest*, C2 had claimed just 0.4 percent of the market. Seven months later, Pepsi announced plans to discontinue Edge. C2 followed quietly. By the summer of 2006, Martin had packed up his desk at 1 Coca-Cola Plaza and left for work at a regional PR outfit.

While Martin was updating his résumé and Coke and Pepsi execs were watching their gilded monstrosities teeter and slip beneath the waves of other new products lapping the shelves in grocery stores around the world, Jones Soda was slapping customers' snapshots on bottles of wild herb stuffing, salmon paté, and pecan pie soda (not to mention a number of standard flavors, like root beer and fruit punch). Jones Soda's revenues grew 70 percent in just two years. Profits climbed into the double digits, and retailers like Starbucks and Target began carrying the label. When limited-edition flavors started fetching $100 on eBay, it was clear that Peter van Stolk's upstart brand had arrived.

Why did the world's number-one brand and its principal rival fall flat on their faces in the summer of 2004? Coke and Pepsi invested millions in market research and employed skilled designers and brand strategists to create their brand architecture from the ground up. But mid-calorie sodas flopped. As the low-carb fad melted away, customers saw no reason to switch from diet or regular to something in between. Meanwhile, van Stolk's strategy at Jones appealed to people. With its funky, offbeat flavors and customer-generated labels, Jones Soda seemed more interested in having fun than forcing anything down people's throats. "What I really wanted to do with the turkey and gravy, I wanted to say we're not afraid to do it," admitted van Stolk. "And now what we're making fun of is the whole carb thing. Now you can have a carb-free turkey-and-gravy dinner. We're just going to hammer away and make it a big, big parody."[1]

If Coke and Pepsi can't afford accurate market research, it simply doesn't exist. If market research works like a charm, it would have pointed Coke and Pepsi toward alternative, ironic flavors rather than the doomed low-carb twins, C2 and Edge. At the very least, the estimates wouldn't have been so high, or the trend projections would have seen the end of the low-carb fad, or executives would have pared back the launch budgets.

Coke and Pepsi are in the dark—and they aren't alone. Knowing which ads will work and which products will sell in a splintering global market becomes more difficult every year. Courted with more choices, already fickle customers become even harder to cater to. Smaller media channels and niches frustrate marketers trying to reach their target markets. C2 and Edge, with their exaggerated projections and multimillion-dollar campaigns, were products of marketers' fantasies and myopia. Yet big brands continue with business as usual, designing products from the outside in—spending millions on surveys and peering into customers' minds, hunting out "unmet needs." But for all the research, identifying the best products and advertisements remains a difficult task that can be accomplished only with true creativity and a genuine feel for the customer's needs.

Questionnaires, two-way mirrors, hidden cameras— you name it, we've been exposed to marketing scrutiny. Gallup's been at it since the 1930s, and sociologist Robert K. Merton hosted the first focus group in 1941. But with some thirty-five thousand new consumer packaged goods hitting grocery store shelves every year,[2] telephone surveys and focus groups have a sad track record for predicting success. Depending on who you ask, no more than 10 percent of new products, and perhaps as few as 1 percent, survive their first year on the market.

In the past few years, a new generation of market researchers has emerged on the branding scene. Waving PhDs, they're encouraging the use of methodology that borrows from research in neuroscience, psychology, and artificial intelligence in an effort to gain insight into how we actually think. The marketing-world equivalent of mapping the human genome, this effort reflects a keener, more accurate brand age. Seductively high-tech and exotic, the new wave of methods has CEOs (only one in five of whom have any marketing experience) anticipating the day they'll be able to track ads and products down the distribution channel, from the factory into our heads. Along the way, they are figuring out which ads work and which ads don't, as well as discovering often disturbing truths about how brands reshape our reality from the inside out.

□   □   □

Coca-Cola isn't just the most popular soft drink on earth. It's the number-one brand on earth, a title it has held undefeated for five years—as long as Interbrand has been statistically ranking the world's top global brands. In 2007 Coke was worth $65.3 billion in brand equity (the estimated value of the brand beyond its tangible assets), easily outpacing other household brand names like Microsoft (number two at $58.7 billion), McDonald's (number eight at $29.4 billion), and Disney (number nine at $29.2 billion). Pepsi—valued at $12.9 billion—limped in at number twenty-six.[3]

And yet Pepsi has been winning blind taste tests since the first "Pepsi Challenge" over thirty years ago. The apparent secret to Coke's success isn't some nineteenth-century pharmacist's formula locked in a safe in Atlanta—it is branding. Pepsi claimed the top spot in the Quebec soda market twenty years ago by hiring local celebrities. After two decades of local advertising, Quebecers don't see Pepsi as the "other" soda; they see it as *their* soda. In America, Coke outsells Pepsi for the same reason—it is anchored deep in our sense of identity.

In 2004 Professor Read Montague, a neuroscientist at the Baylor College of Medicine in Houston, Texas, published a landmark neurological study of Pepsi and Coke that showed that the *idea* of Coke was powerful enough to override people's sense of taste.[4] Half of the test subjects preferred Pepsi in blind taste tests. When they were asked to try a second round of taste tests, this time without the blindfolds, Coke won over 75 percent of the subjects. Studying the results, Montague concluded that the act of seeing the Coke label had activated the area of the brain associated with self-image and cultural identity. The subjects identified with Coke. Despite what their taste buds told them, Coke's brand was stronger. Their brains were effectively ignoring taste in order to cling to the proverbial security blanket.

Most of us can find ways to rationalize purchases; we often ignore our better sense when we shell out extra cash for brand-name items for which there are less expensive alternatives of equal quality. All it takes is an endorsement from Oprah and we stampede each other for $280 cashmere pet clothing. But Montague's findings point to something more sinister: that a *feeling* about a brand can eclipse an honest, taste-driven response. Years of ads can corrupt the intelligence of the senses.

It would be reasonable to assume that the people in Atlanta who are in the soda business might have regarded the results of Montague's study as a backhanded compliment. At the heart of Coke's success is image, and yet again, here was image trumping product. Coke spent $740 million on advertising in 2006, but just pennies per gallon on ingredients.[5] Its product is as much on the can as in it.

□   □   □

Three years after Montague published his study, the immature field he thrust into the international spotlight is burgeoning with entrepreneurial neuroscientists. Some leave academia directly for cushy contracts at ad firms, some hang up their own shingle, and others take posts inside brands. Private companies like Neuroco and Neurosense in England and BrightHouse in Georgia have attracted headlines for work on projects as diverse as public transit in Atlanta to analyzing consumers' responses to camera ads for Hewlett-Packard. But this is just the tip of the iceberg; neuromarketing is still a nascent industry.

"Right now we're doing astronomy with binoculars," says Roger Dooley, a marketing executive. "Over time we'll get to the high-powered telescope." Dooley is the founder of Neurosciencemarketing.com, a website that highlights developments in the field. He estimates that 5 to 10 percent of the Fortune 500 have sampled neuromarketing, though it's hard to know for sure because results are kept private. Dooley anticipates more brands entering the market as the technology improves. "They're saying, 'We may look foolish down the road, but we're going to try it,'" he says. "And of course, you have folks out there watching this and making hokum claims."

A neuroscientist and kung fu black belt, Dr. Lawrence Farwell has worked as a consultant to the CIA, a commercial real estate agent, and a transcendental meditation instructor. Once a research associate at Harvard Medical School, he has taught at Maharishi International University, the institution founded by the disgraced guru once beloved by the Beatles. The son of physicist George Farwell—one of the few elite scientists handpicked to work alongside Enrico Fermi on the Manhattan Project—Farwell is lean and angular with an easy smile and a loose mop of brown hair. Known for his antics, he once staged a kung fu battle before a class of undergraduates.

Farwell studied for his PhD under noted cognitive psychophysiologist and former NASA researcher Emanuel

Donchin at the University of Illinois at Urbana-Champaign. His findings, reported in a paper coauthored with Donchin about how the brain reacts electrically when it recognizes particular pieces of information, are stunning. When guilty subjects were presented with an incriminating article of evidence in a mock-trail scenario, their brains generated a distinct electrical pattern visible to the trained eye on an electroencephalogram (EEG).

When CIA officials wanted to know if Farwell's technique—called MERMER (memory- and encoding-related multifaceted electroencephalographic response)—could be used to read minds, they signed their first $1 million deal with him.

Farwell spent three years working as a CIA consultant, during which time he collaborated with the FBI and the Navy on a number of MERMER studies. Though Farwell considers his early work with the agency successful (he used MERMER to identify U.S. Navy medics and FBI agents hidden among anonymous subjects), the CIA did not extend his contract. Several years later, the *Des Moines Register* quoted an assistant director at the FBI who discredited Farwell's work for being inconclusive and below the Bureau's standards.

After his stint with the CIA, Farwell dedicated years to applying MERMER to law enforcement cases; he claimed, for instance, that his application was used to help clear the name of a Virginia police officer accused of drug dealing and to establish the innocence of a convicted murderer in

Iowa. Convicts around the country appealed for Farwell's help, and by 2004 he had built up a backlog of some four hundred cases—many of them death row inmates. Criticism has dogged Farwell, and skeptics, including judges, fellow psychophysiologists, and his former dissertation adviser, have been easy to find. In recent years, Farwell has enlisted MERMER for less noble causes. On a given afternoon, one might find him trying to determine the emotional resonance of different brands of cleaning products.

Brain Fingerprinting Laboratories, Farwell's company, has helped brands better understand their customers by analyzing the electrical signals in their brains after they've watched commercials. Farwell uses a computer to measure the brain's response to a certain word, phrase, image, or sound. Through MERMER analysis, Farwell claims he can tell whether the information was previously stored in the subject's brain. In measuring a subject's response to TV commercials, Farwell can determine what kinds of ads activate and excite the brain, what kind are more likely to be retained, and what kind are capable of making lasting impressions. After researching neuroscience in relation to criminal justice and medicine for twenty years, it is perhaps unsurprising that Farwell landed in branding. But he owes his thanks to Eileen Campbell.

Eileen Campbell is the CEO of Millward Brown Group, a leading international market research company that specializes in "helping companies maximize their brand equity, brand performance and brand health"; currently Millward Brown works with 70 percent of the world's top brands. Campbell and Farwell linked up in 2005 as part of Millward Brown's effort to better understand how emotions can be used to strengthen brands' bonds with consumers. "People can use a million words, but there are really about twenty core emotions," she explains. What Farwell confirmed by studying subjects' brain waves was that tapping into emotions is the way to build stronger brands.

In Brain Fingerprinting Laboratories' first study for Millward Brown, subjects who had seen an ad displayed a MERMER in response to some parts of the ad but not to others. The product being advertised, a bathroom cleaning product, received no signal from key areas of subjects' brains.

While the brand fell short, the researchers at Brain Fingerprinting Laboratories learned an important branding lesson. The tests revealed that when an ad portrays two people interacting closely (hugging, for instance), the MERMER comes through loud and clear. "We found that human interaction made a tremendous impact," says Farwell. "But the product in this ad was not connected to the human interaction, so it didn't make an impression." The implication for brand strategists is clear: while most bathroom cleaning ads would naturally appeal to the functional assets of the brand—ease of use, greater effectiveness than the competitor's product—what really connects with viewers at home is the level of emotion associated with any given product.

In her response to these results, Campbell admits that it's a mixed bag. "Some are really intrigued," she says of Millward Brown's clients. "Some find it utterly creepy." And she readily admits that there's a *1984*-ish quality to the work. "It's a sexy tool with a lot of future uses. . . . [However,] if someone told me they were going to analyze my brain waves for brand recall, I'd tell them it sounds creepy too." Then, after a moment's hesitation, she hastens to add, "That's Eileen Campbell the human being talking, not Eileen Campbell the Millward Brown executive."

□   □   □

The man who holds the original patent on neuroimaging marketing is Gerald Zaltman, a seasoned Harvard Business School professor and author of *How Customers Think*. During the 1990s, Zaltman and Stephen Kozzlyn, chair of Harvard's psychology department, did several pilot studies with brain scans to study how people think about certain consumer experiences like buying a car. When people were asked to imagine a car salesman, blood flowed to areas of the brain associated with negative feelings. Asked to imagine a better car dealership, the brain scans reflected positive, calming feelings.

"Nine out of ten don't realize it, but every one of these neuromarketing companies is infringing on my dad's patent," says Lindsay Zaltman. But Zaltman is happy, according to his son, to see his work making a difference. Neuroimaging, an expensive technique that requires that subjects ingest barium liquid to illuminate brain flow, didn't interest Zaltman personally. Instead of using machines to scan brains, Gerald and Lindsay Zaltman devoted themselves to plumbing the depths of our unconscious minds by way of the Zaltman Metaphor Elicitation Technique (ZMET), a form of psychoanalysis that borrows from neurobiology, linguistics, and art theory. In research sessions, the Zaltmans interview subjects, aiming to draw out images and feelings capable of elucidating insights and responses that the subject may not have been able to verbalize.

Research suggests that 80 percent of human communication is nonverbal. Digging deeper with ZMET involves a concerted focus on the core metaphors, known as "the seven giants," that every human being uses to understand the world and communicate with others—balance, connection, container, control, journey, resource, and transformation. Subjects might, for example, bring in a picture of an airplane to help describe how the atmosphere at a chain of Chinese-food restaurants transported them to another world, or an image of a butterfly to represent personal transformation. One recent client, a major candy manufacturer, was curious about what consumers really thought about gum. Rather than asking gum chewers to rate their favorite brand, as would happen in surveys or focus groups, the Zaltmans might ask, "If you were a stick of chewing gum, what would you tell the world about yourself?"

The results of the Zaltmans' five-country gum study are being used to develop the next generation of gum ads, flavors, and names. Interestingly, it is the stereotypically duller industries—IT, pharmaceuticals, B2B (business-to-business) banking—that get the most excited about the ZMET results. "They feel like their consumers are emotionless, that they just want to know how well products work," says Lindsay Zaltman. "But people really open up. IT employees talk about how they might lose their job if the software doesn't work. We've had doctors cry in interviews."

It may not sound like the kind of work that would earn you tenure in the Ivy League, let alone a foot in the door at any major business, but the companies that have tapped the Zaltmans' firm, Olsen Zaltman Associates (OZA), in hopes of plugging into customers' "windows of consciousness" include Coca-Cola, P&G, GM, Nestlé, and General Mills. Sixty percent of OZA's total business is with global brands. In the past several years, the company has expanded from eight employees to twenty-five, and revenues have kept pace, pushing 20 to 30 percent growth a year.

Proud of the track record of ZMET's low-tech psychoanalysis, Lindsay Zaltman cautions companies that are considering the use of the latest developments in neuromarketing. The field is growing quickly, and there are a lot of new companies with little experience. "Nowadays it doesn't take anything to offer these services up with some flashy language," he says. "Unwitting clients will walk right into it."

□ □ □

How our brains respond to information isn't the only thing that interests marketers: some are now hiring experts in facial responses and expressions. Dan Hill's job—and that of his company Sensory Logic—is literally to read faces. A fleeting ripple in the flesh of the forehead, a slight flaring of the nostrils, a barely perceptible pursing of the lips—such is the currency of his trade. Taking measurements to the tenths and hundredths of a second, Hill translates facial expressions for executives at companies like PetSmart, Nextel, Target, and GlaxoSmithKline.

Using video recordings and electromyography—a process that monitors tiny electrical signals released by muscle contractions—Hill reads the movements of people's facial muscles (there are forty-three of these muscles) while they watch TV. It's the kind of job that requires deep reserves of patience and an incredible attention to detail. Spotting an activated zygomatic major (one of the muscles that controls the mouth) while a viewer is watching a commercial is a bad sign. But Hill can help.

In 1998, while at work on the branding task force at a utility company in New Jersey, Hill was inspired by an article about the role of emotions in people's decisions and considered doing market research on the subject. But as he's now fond of saying, "You can't ask people to think their feelings."

Questionnaires with fill-in-the-bubble responses like "very satisfied" and "somewhat dissatisfied" fail to capture much in the way of true emotion. Meanwhile, asking people in focus groups about their emotional response to an ad or a product offers only a rough approximation. The ego and superego are crappy lobbyists when it comes to convincing us to buy stuff. Like schoolmarms, they quibble over rational considerations and shush the impulsive stimulus triggered by emotion. What Hill needed was a direct line to the id. When he read that people born blind exhibit the same facial expressions as everyone else, he knew he'd found it.

"This looked to me like the intellectual gold rush of the era," says Hill of stumbling upon facial coding at his local library. "I knew I'd come upon something that could go across ethnic, gender, and cultural boundaries." The human face—responsible for about 50 percent of our physical communication—is a highly specialized tool through which we subconsciously relay to the world much of what's going on inside our heads. It is in fact the only area of the body where our muscles connect directly to our skin and allow us to display emotion with an infinite dexterity.

Hill draws much of his understanding of faces from Paul Ekman, a psychology professor who pioneered the physiology of emotion in the 1960s. Ekman is the author of the Facial Action Coding System (FACS), a five-hundred-page taxonomy of some three thousand unique expressions. FACS has proven to be widely applicable, everywhere from the Department of Defense's advanced research arm, DARPA, to animation studios.

For Sensory Logic to make a legitimate claim that it could divine people's thoughts and emotions from tiny facial tics, Ekman was key. With his help, Hill was able to develop a facial coding system. Since then, he's become a recognized expert in the field.

In one test, subjects of a Sensory Logic study sit in front of a television screen and are wired with a finely tuned electrode that reads the corrugator muscle, located just above the eyebrows in the middle forehead. Hill used to place a clip on the subject's finger to measure galvanic skin response, a means of discerning the individual's state of stress or arousal by way of the conductivity of sweat produced by tiny glands in the skin, but now he uses an eye-tracking method that he has found to be a better determinant of the parts of a commercial that are appealing to the subject.

Otherwise known as "tells" in poker, so-called hits, or an individual's distinct tics, can correspond to what Hill calls "the six-pack of core emotions": happiness, anger, disgust, fear, sadness, and surprise. The objective in observing these hits is to determine a subject's true feelings about everything from a commercial voice-over to the company logo. Hill has made a successful career out of reading faces. In 2003 Target executives called on him when they were deciding whether to sell Dayton's department store; the *New York Times* approached him to analyze George Bush's and John Kerry's faces during their 2004 presidential campaigns; and more recently, the Discovery Channel flew him to Las Vegas to read poker players' tells. Networks like CNN have relied on Hill to read candidates' countenances during the 2008 presidential campaign. Once, an investment firm even asked Hill to analyze the faces of various CEOs to determine who was the most trustworthy.

In 1999, when U-Haul was rethinking its company logo, it approached Hill for help in determining which of the three prototypes best fit its company profile. One logo featured a price tag, one an image of the road, and one an image of a U-Haul truck. Though the sign with the price tag and the one with the ubiquitous U-Haul truck were direct and simple, they flopped. But the third—with its softened cartoon lanes vanishing over the horizon— promised something more: opportunity, adventure, the open road. Faces lit up.

Granted, the promise doesn't exactly fit the product. While moving is arguably a liberating experience, for most of us driving a rented moving van is not. Although maneuvering a cumbersome, gas-guzzling truck with a swimming-pool-size blind spot on and off freeways and through narrow city streets is something of a rite of passage in the United States, it's one that most of us would prefer to avoid. So why did the third sign—the one hanging above 14,500 locations around the world today[6]—elicit a better response than signs that appealed to reason and simplicity? According to Hill, "it's not enough to be on message. You have to be on emotion."

Although business at Sensory Logic is growing, a recent development at MIT's Media Lab is taking the field in an entirely automated direction. Pioneering the use of machines and software in the name of reading faces, Rana el Kaliouby might just put Hill, Ekman, and every other facial coder out of work.

□   □   □

If you've seen *Minority Report*, Steven Spielberg's adaptation of Philip K. Dick's classic sci-fi story, you probably remember the futuristic lasers that scan Tom Cruise's irises at every turn, simultaneously serving up slick ads for Guinness and American Express. In crowded malls and trams, they call out Cruise's name as he runs by. An Orwellian vision of the future, *Minority Report* left audiences buzzing with what-ifs. What if technology advanced to the point where advertisements peered back at us? What if they could read our faces and assess our moods? Would they send us ads for coffee when we look tired, or commercials for antidepressants if we look blue? What if the technology already existed?

Each April, representatives from multinational corporations arrive in Cambridge, Massachusetts, at the Body Sensor Network Conference to talk about the future of technology and health care. Shaking off the morning chill, corporate executives take their seats alongside academics from the world's leading universities to discuss the latest medical technologies that promise to someday save lives and improve our standard of living. The conference schedule is packed with odd and promising work, ranging from the auspicious to the outrageous. (A professor from Brown University is slated to speak on a "Direct Brain Interface to Restore Function in Humans with Spinal Cord Injury," and researchers from Germany are sharing their findings on a "Sensory Baby Vest for the Monitoring of Infants.") Intended to save lives as well as improve the quality of life, the research presented by the conference participants seems a far cry from branding.

For a woman with a PhD in computer science, Rana el Kaliouby spends a lot of time looking at faces. While other programmers work with bits and bytes, El Kaliouby deals in smiles, nods, and winks. At the 2006 Body Sensor Network Conference, El Kaliouby, an MIT research associate, informed researchers and journalists of a mind-reading machine called the Emotional Social intelligence Prosthesis—ESP for short. Using video cameras and complex algorithms, the device monitors tiny changes in a person's facial expression—a skeptically arched eyebrow, say, or an impatient tenseness to the lips—and provides an instantaneous assessment of the individual's mental state. Instead of spitting out ads, however, ESP will be used to assist sufferers of autism (many of whom have difficulty understanding social cues) by helping them recognize how others are feeling.

Following el Kaliouby's presentation, the press buzzed about MIT scientists who had developed a "mind-reading device." While el Kaliouby emphasized that she was focused on applying her research to people with disabilities, Peter Robinson, her professor at Cambridge, had a different answer for journalists. The leading authority on mind-reading machines, Robinson alluded to one possible use of such technology: websites that could receive data through a webcam and tailor advertising or product offerings to a person's mood. In essence, TV watching you.

□   □   □

But are better, more tailored ads better for us? Gary Ruskin, the tireless executive director of Ralph Nader's Commercial Alert, doesn't think so. "Americans are already suffering from an epidemic of marketing-related diseases," he says. "Smoking, gambling, obesity—any marginal gain in the effectiveness of marketing could be devastating to public health." (The national lottery in the United Kingdom has already begun neuromarketing research.)

Researchers at the Harvard School of Public Health estimate that smoking results in 4.83 million premature deaths a year worldwide. In the United States, that number is about 400,000, or 45 deaths every hour. A mere 2 percent increase in the effectiveness of cigarette marketing would result in 8,000 added deaths each year—a net result of about one more death per hour.

The biggest hurdle to getting the message across in Washington is the ignorance that goes hand in hand with this uncharted territory. After several years of calls and letters, a congressional hearing on the ethics of neuromarketing will be inevitable.

Who can blame brands for leveraging emotion more precisely to their advantage? If ads and packaging that romance our id are what sell, companies will do whatever it takes. As Nigel Hollis, Millward Brown's chief global analyst, explains it, "Everybody is looking for the magic bullet, and we can't afford not to look too."

But a world full of advertisers pampering our inner child won't be a pretty place. In the past, we have experienced our emotions largely on our own terms. Sure, the occasional ad for Kodak or fabric softener might have tugged at our heartstrings. But if every advertisement, no matter the product, is looking to land a direct punch to our emotional sweet spot, the only recourse will be to develop thicker skin. More important, brands like Coke and Pepsi—as obsessed with research and branding as they are—can't tap into the kind of emotional resonance that Jones Soda strikes with customers. As it stands, neuroscience may yet trump gut instinct and market research. When that day comes, our obsessive branding disorder will devolve even further. With the keys to our brains, the same brands that slip product placements into our favorite programs and employ word-of-mouth marketers to make underhanded pitches to our neighbors will take advantage of the latest research neuroscientists have to offer.

Getting
Personal

In order to be successful, one must project
an image of success at all times.

—American Beauty, 1999

n May 2004, the U.S. Patent and Trademark Office published a series of trademarks awarded to pop singer
Christina Aguilera. Aguilera (or more likely her agent)
had submitted a list of hundreds of products to be marketed under her name. The application included 450 imagined goods or services—almost half as many as Thomas
Edison's record-setting 1,093 patents—ranging from the
mundane (body gels, panty hose) to the outlandish (badminton sets, modeling clay). The former Mouseketeer envisioned customers wearing Aguilera-branded contact
lenses, drawing with Aguilera crayons, playing with an
Aguilera badminton set, and freshening up with an
Aguilera antiperspirant.[1]

In 2006 celebrity-licensed products accounted for an estimated $3 billion in U.S. sales.[2] Twenty-five percent of all ads now feature a celebrity—twice the percentage in 1995.[3] There's even a formula that companies can use to determine how effective a particular celebrity's endorsement might be for their products. Developed by the L.A. marketing agency Davie Brown Entertainment, the Davie-Brown Index is a branding matrix of 1,500 celebrities backed by an ongoing survey of 1.5 million consumers. Respondents are asked to rank celebrities on eight criteria: appeal, notice, trendsetting, influence, trust, endorsement, aspiration, and awareness. Davie-Brown sells annual subscriptions to the index to advertisers and brands for $20,000.

But even as the metrics grow more precise, celebrity endorsements have gotten more inane. What's to stop a pop star from tapping into the top-forty, teenage-girl, badminton market if George Foreman can successfully hawk plug-in grills (over 80 million sold) and Sylvester Stallone can pitch his own brand of high-protein pudding (in milk chocolate, vanilla, and banana crème flavor)? Such is the nature of celebrity brands, where the name comes before the product. Fashion designer Vera Wang made her name with glamorous wedding dresses. Today she also has a line of mattresses. Chuck Norris and James Belushi have their own brand of cigars and cigar-related accessories; Donald Trump has a cologne, and Mariah Carey a Zinfandel. What is most notable about Aguilera's trademark application isn't the ambitious range of items she imagined selling, but that she imagined selling those items herself. She wasn't waiting around for GNC to license her name for a new formula of diet pills, or for Crayola to petition her for product placement in one of her videos. Instead, Aguilera was laying the foundation for a global lifestyle brand—shoelaces, shot glasses, sex toys, and all.

With major celebrities, it's difficult to tell where the product stops and the person begins. The brand equity of major celebrities (think Oprah) is inseparable from their personal lives, which are documented in breathless detail in the magazines lining supermarket checkout aisles around the world. Having jumped from products to celebrities, it was only a matter of time before branding trickled down to the average citizen. In the process, a promotional tactic devised to sell inanimate products has evolved into a life strategy adopted by millions of people around the world. New generations are already growing up indoctrinated in an age of marketing determined to reshape us.

As the personal branding phenomenon works itself deeper into the fabric of modern life, it's warping how we see each other, and how we see ourselves. Consumers have become enamored with reinventing themselves. Americans spent some $10 billion on self-help books, motivational speakers, and related self-improvement products in 2007, and analysts expect the market to grow by another $1 billion in 2008.[4] Meanwhile, reality makeover shows, appealing to every niche and demographic, are ubiquitous. Beyond the radical image makeovers, like those seen on *Extreme Makeover*, *What Not to Wear*, and *Trick My Trucker*, we've come to demand instant behavioral transformations too, be it from our pets (*The Dog Whisperer*), our families (*Shalom in the Home*), or our children (*Nanny 911*, *Supernanny*).

Personal branding didn't spread this far and this fast without a little help, of course. Rising from strip malls, office parks, and every corner of the Web, self-proclaimed specialists have rushed to bring the methods to the masses. Some see it as a novel career tool, others as a new-age ideology. Either way, such initiatives are about as common as Bic lighters and are available for hire in every midsized town in the United States. Accessible and affordable personal branding is here to stay; the phenomenon comes hand in hand with our media-saturated culture, in which, to embrace a common understanding of success, we are encouraged to think of ourselves as akin to products more than as emotive human beings.

□ □ □

Most of today's personal branding experts range somewhere between corny and culty. Medicine men, motivational speakers, and etiquette specialists, they sell naive customers advice on what to wear, how to shake hands, and even how to stand while waiting for their luggage at baggage claim. Tom Peters is different. One of the original rock stars of the industry, his message is fairly simple: "We are CEOs of our own companies: Me Inc."

A consultant and management expert, Peters introduced much of the world to personal branding with the 1997 *Fast Company* cover story "The Brand Called You." In it, Peters encouraged entrepreneurs to better their professional and personal lives by thinking of themselves as brands. His article played no small role in shifting how people understood branding and helped fuel the free-agent revolution of the dot-com era by inspiring people to strike out on their own. The implications of Peters's personal branding philosophy were both promising and puzzling. By subscribing to a business approach that took its cues from established products, people felt somehow more alive. Applied to the individual, corporate requirements like developing mission statements and determining asset allocation became inspiring. People envisioned their own metamorphoses in a manner similar to a company rolling out a new logo. Peters's conceit—that we too can benefit from the tried-and-true rules of salesmanship—landed him a book deal, and he was soon being courted for lectures around the country.

Inundated with fan mail, Peters took his show on the road. In front of conference rooms packed with eager entrepreneurs, he hammered his mantra home: We are brands. At the end of the day, the word is you. Audiences loved the sound of it.

Personal branding is appealing for as many reasons as there are people who have tried it. But the sense of empowerment that personal branding offers is something to which almost all attest. Peters called on his budding branders to project an image of strength and clarity by mimicking the corporate products they most admired.

Riding the personal branding tidal wave, Peters become one of the most successful business personalities alive. *Fortune* called him an "ur-guru" (*The Economist* opted for uber-guru); National Public Radio named his book, *In Search of Excellence*, one of the "top three business books of the century." His outfit, the Tom Peters Company, has offices in Boston, London, and Manchester, Vermont. Curiously, there's little mention of personal branding on his website today.

While Peters jump-started personal branding, he left us to carry out his mission. In many cases, the story of the personal branding craze was pretty much the same: a person was inspired, quit work, launched a web company, courted the venture capital firms for money, leased a BMW until the bubble popped, then returned to work. By 2002, the personal branding fad was fading fast. But the industry refused to die.

Since their brief heyday in the late 1990s, a handful of resolute disciples have continued to proselytize. Personal branding books (*U R a Brand!*, *Self-Marketing Power*) continue to crop up regularly on Amazon, CEOs still occasionally sign up for a personal branding session with a reigning guru, and tens of thousands of rank-and-file workers around the world line up annually for a regimented diet of canned optimism and connect-the-dot formulas.

□   □   □

Unsatisfied with their image and unsure what do about it, consumers in the market for personal branding are generally comforted by the idea of a step-by-step branding formula. Much in the manner that LPK creates a simple-to-follow "Tool Box Vision" to help "develop and support the atmosphere" of Froot Loops, personal branding gurus provide their clients with organized processes for developing their brands and reshaping their lives and careers. Some, like Derek Armstrong, have leaned heavily on a formulaic approach to getting the results they're after.

Armstrong, a Canadian marketing executive with nearly three decades of experience in advertising and branding, has been manufacturing image for individuals since the early 1980s. Though not quite a celebrity himself, if you're willing to follow one of his formulas, he might be able to turn you into one. His company, Persona Corporation, has branded hundreds of professionals around the world. By Armstrong's count, he has a 97.6 percent success rate (as measured against clients' marketing objectives). He attributes this success to the multitude of acronym-laden systems and programs offered by his company.

Though one of the most appealing aspects of developing a personal brand is the organized method, when we scratch the surface we find that many personal branding systems, much like self-help programs and get-rich-quick schemes, are quite complex. To map Armstrong's ever-expanding formulas, methodologies, codes, and tools requires an entire book: *The Persona Principle: How to Succeed in Business with Image-Marketing*.

Each year Persona performs an in-depth examination of sixty-two industries, from music and computers to publishing and commodities companies. Persona distinguishes within this variegated landscape five principal personality types: Emperor (think globally dominant Coca-Cola), Hero (Apple the innovator), Expert (esteemed chef Mario Batali), Buddy (Charles Schwab's "Chuck"), and the most dynamic, Simpatico (Richard Branson and Virgin). Each personality type has ninety-six key attributes, including a person's name, target audience, and credibility. The more closely a person's attributes align with one of the five defined personality types, the better his or her chances (according to Armstrong's calculation) of branded success.

In addition to image equity, individuals are also measured on the Credibility Equity Index, which slots them into one of four categories: John Q. Public, Politics, Hollywood, or Corporate. Each carries a distinct degree of credibility and visibility. All told, clients often require a year of dutiful study and analysis before they're considered brand-ready. Sometimes reshaping the personality takes a lot longer.

"We have something called the Rule of Five," Armstrong says, explaining the evolution of the process. "If you can't own one of the five personalities within five years, you either have to niche down or you'll go out of business." In essence, to "niche down" translates to adjusting your goals. First, all of Armstrong's clients aspire to be Experts. When it becomes clear that this may be too ambitious (or too expensive, or too time-consuming), Persona Corporation specialists might counsel clients to niche down to the Buddy category.

As complex and time-consuming as the process can be, Armstrong's goal is for each of his clients to be recognized for a single thing. This proves especially helpful in the publishing industry. Armstrong starts the personal branding process with authors by looking for something sensational—a memorable element of the book or the writer. In many cases, the hook involves positioning an author behind his or her most contentious idea.

When he was hired to help launch Cheryl Kaye Tardif's young adult novel *Whale Song*, Armstrong capitalized on the sinister backstory of the protagonist's daughter, who assists in her mother's suicide. By effectively positioning a character in *Whale Song* as an advocate of assisted suicide, Armstrong elevated Tardif's novel beyond its fictional boundaries into the contentious social dialogue over euthanasia. Left to her own devices, it's unlikely that Tardif would have chosen this course. But the point of personal branding is to be noticed and remembered, not to be yourself.

After helping authors find their particular niche, Armstrong works with them to build their online personality. Accordingly, their online brand is also intended to be memorable, since few readers will ever see the author in person. Before his authors do appear in public for readings, Armstrong takes great care to ensure that they don't break from the brand—even going so far as to determine what clothes they should wear.

The personal brand most commonly backfires when an artist "violates" the brand by heading in a new direction. But by and large, Armstrong's clients are willing to listen. As he sees it, they wouldn't be knocking on his door in the first place if they weren't unsatisfied with their identity.

On the other side of the personal branding coin is its sinister inverse: a psychological approach to understanding companies as though they themselves were sympathetic individuals. Dr. Kerry Sulkowicz, a psychologist and psychoanalyst who teaches clinical psychiatry, has devoted his career to the growing field of business psychology in which companies are personified or analyzed like people.

As a self-described "psychoanalytic management consultant," it would stand to reason that Sulkowicz would be just as comfortable discussing personal branding as he is talking about personified brands, but while the two concepts mirror each other, they are nothing alike. Examining a corporation as if it were a person, we can imbue that company with a distinct personality and soul. Understood this way, it's easier to imagine what a brand might feel, say, or do in a certain situation. While an intriguing experiment, such anthropomorphizing of a company offers a shallow and depressing understanding of humanity. Turn the same lens on the individual and, as Sulkowicz puts it, "there is something inherently deeply cynical about turning a complex human being into something like Kleenex."

And yet this is exactly what personal branding is—conceptualizing an individual as a product on a shelf and strategizing how best to market that product to the world. But personal branding isn't a theoretical exercise—it's a symptom of a chronic cultural disorder resulting from society's prolonged overexposure to branding.

□   □   □

In 2002, when Peter Montoya lured people with an energizing can-do attitude toward self-fulfillment, he encouraged his clients to see themselves as idealized visions of their own brands, the so-called brand called you. Montoya's spiel couldn't have been more promising. Pictured in a black V-neck sweater, Montoya invited his online visitors to "join the Personal Branding revolution," enroll in his Personal Branding University, and "plug yourself into supercharged growth" with a subscription to *Personal Branding* magazine.

Montoya's first heavily touted book, *The Brand Called You*, was published in 1997 during the heady days of the dot-com boom, and it quickly elevated him to stardom. Personal branding, Montoya promised, was "the most powerful business success tool ever devised." And he believed it too. In the early days he was so confident that personal branding would take the world by storm that he sold his house to keep the business running. His bet paid off.

Since founding his company in 2001, Montoya and his colleagues (known as "The Brand Called Michelle Volz," "The Brand Called Nick Ray," and so on) have guided more than two thousand people through the Peter Montoya Inc. personal branding process. In 2002, riding the wave of his first book, he launched a quarterly, *Peter Montoya's Personal Branding*, and published *The Personal Branding Phenomenon*. The revolution was under way.

In a field overrun with self-declared experts but few proven stars, Montoya's widespread success has lent the personal branding industry a sense of legitimacy. Suddenly, Montoya became the leading expert, the sage guru who could distinguish good personal branding from bad. According to him, the business community doesn't really understand what personal branding is about. "Mention it to twenty professionals—you'll get excitement, but no idea what it really is," he says. "Is it your hairstyle? Sure.

How you talk? That's part of it. By and large, though, personal branding is misunderstood by most coaches and business professionals in the industry."

As Montoya sees it, personal branding is about simplifying aspects of an individual's personality to create an aura that is both consistent and unique. The more a person can simplify who he is and what he does, the easier it will be for others to understand, remember, and—most importantly—buy his brand. "Here in the United States we define people by what they do," says Montoya. "Your product, your service, your target market—in personal branding we refine and define these."

The personal branding process at Peter Montoya Inc. begins by helping clients home in on the right personal aspects and audiences, limiting what they sell about themselves (a process that closely resembles Armstrong's "niche-ing down"). When helping a client develop her personal brand, Montoya might encourage her to begin highlighting her most profitable skill rather than emphasize her diverse set of talents. The same principle applies to examining her customers. He advises her to cater to the most profitable one-third of her customers, not the other 66 percent. Once these limits are established, the personal slogan comes into play.

Slogans are touchy territory for brands—especially when they're representative of an individual. Although they offer an opportunity to encapsulate a broad mission in a terse, easy-to-remember statement, slogans are often simply too narrow or vague—as evidenced by the largely forgettable city- and state-brand slogans adopted around the world in recent years. Iconic companies like Nike ("Just Do It") and Apple ("Think Different") can get away with vagueness because consumers already know what they do. Individuals looking to develop a distinct personal brand don't have the same liberty. From where Montoya sits, brand slogans must be immediate and straightforward—often a tall order when a client is seeking a pitch-perfect tagline.

Once clients have settled on a specific skill set, a narrow market audience, and a snappy slogan, Montoya and his colleagues help them roll out their personal brand—from printing up brochures and stationery to designing a website to creating a marketing timeline. It's a successful formula, one that helped distinguish Montoya early on and continues to attract clients despite the fact that he no longer emphasizes personal branding on his website and in his promotional materials. (*Peter Montoya's Personal Branding* magazine hasn't been published since early 2004, and the website no longer provides links to his Personal Branding University.)

Following in the footsteps of Peters and Montoya, William Arruda has now assumed the crown in the personal branding domain—and he's building an army. The president of Reach Communications Consultancy ("the Human Branding Company"), Arruda has licensed more than 150 personal branding coaches in his "1–2–3 Success! Personal Branding Process" since he founded the company in 2000. His empire stretches across the United States and as far afield as the Bahamas, Indonesia, and South Africa.

Though Peters and Montoya have ceded their territory voluntarily, Arruda says it wasn't for lack of customers needing guidance. "Most executives are still so un-self-aware," he says, a mix of awe and pity in his voice. "They have a hard time understanding who they are."

In addition to executives, many entry- and mid-level workers also have difficulty understanding who they are. "You do a one-day workshop and people are jumping up and down and you've changed their lives, they're so moti-vated and excited," Arruda says. "The next day they're back to the way they were." To address this challenge head on, Arruda has developed annual workshops for dozens of employees at large corporations like Ogilvy and JP Morgan. Six to eight weeks in length, these workshops account for two-thirds of his work.

Like Armstrong's complex formulas at Persona Corpo-ration, some of Arruda's "1–2–3 Success!" program in-volves parsing character traits and skills into dozens of categories. There's even a "weakness section," where coworkers point out each other's flaws. Generally, how-ever, Arruda's process involves focusing on skills and simplifying how they're presented. "All brands are known for something, not a thousand things," he says. "Volvo is 'Safety.' You have to focus."

□   □   □

The rise of personal branding has especially affected professionals who must now compete for clients, like business coaches and career counselors. Mark Hovind is the president and CEO of Jobbait.com, a company devoted to helping white-collar executives land work. For anywhere from $5,000 to $15,000, he'll help clients target their job searches, assemble their résumés, and contact key decision-makers in their industry. Lately, he's noticed a rise in the number of competitors offering to transform customers into brands in order to help them land a job.

From where he sits, Hovind sees personal branding as so much fluff and fuss—ostentatious ornamentation at a premium price. "All they do is wrap language around what the applicant does," he says. "But executives don't have lots of time. When that applicant walks into the CEO's office, the first question is going to be 'Where's the beef?'"

Without question, many personal branding firms take advantage of jargon inflation—essentially charging hundreds of dollars more to "leverage the client's 'brand essence'" in the client's search for a job when a career counselor or an executive search firm would help that person find the same job for less money. The branding process itself varies widely from firm to firm. At Brandego.com, one of the leaders in online personal branding (and a company Arruda helped launch), job seekers are asked to assemble a creative brief to help them discover their brand, complete with images, colors, and audio and video clips.

In contrast to his younger competition, Hovind doesn't strive to brand himself as a guru. His website is plain and simple, his hair is plain-cut and gray, and his polo shirts are plainer still. A veteran of the manufacturing industry, he's worked with composites and plastic injection molding, handled piggyback trailers for Transamerica, and spent two years working in Saudi Arabia for Aremco. After dabbling in direct mail while looking for consulting work in the 1990s, he was asked to help with direct-mail campaigns. In 2002 he founded Jobbait.com.

Though he's substantially more expensive than online job sites and the average personal branding specialist, Hovind offers an 85 percent success rate in placing clients at jobs within three months. None of Hovind's clients are branded in the process. As he sees it, the cookie-cutter branding techniques employed by many personal branders can actually impair some job seekers. "They focus their clients on what they do best and structure everything around that," he says. While it's generally not a problem, this approach won't help job seekers who have worked at one company for their entire career or are trying to find work in a shrinking industry.

One of Hovind's clients was a textiles executive in Charlotte, North Carolina. Had he sent his materials off to an online personal branding site, he likely would have been required to state his objective (to get a job in textiles) and to emphasize his stellar career as an expert in textiles. Hovind's solution was more nuanced. "This guy was making $475,000 base pay, with an annual bonus of up to a million bucks," he says. "But there's no future in textiles; the industry has lost more jobs than any other." Though his client hadn't considered switching industries, it was in his best interest, Hovind thought, to look for experience that might offer a way out of textiles. When Hovind discovered that his client had spearheaded several turnaround operations throughout his career, he helped him emphasize *this* experience to land a high-paying job in a different field.

Specifics and hard data are conspicuously absent from a lot of "branded" résumés and profiles, which generally play up language over data. At Brandego.com, any material incorporating a statistic is lumped together toward the middle or end of a job seeker's portfolio. Most personal branding specialists started in idea-driven fields like marketing and advertising, the results of which can be difficult to measure and are often unreliable. Coming out of manufacturing, Hovind's eye is always on the bottom line, on the tangible, quantifiable facts. If an executive is still interested in an applicant after the bottom line has been conveyed, then it's fine to move on to the softer stuff. Professionally, Hovind understands personal branding as putting the cart before the horse.

Personally, the implications are more troubling. Any attempt to market people inevitably runs up against a wall. The clearest, most effective way to communicate and keep people's attention is to condense a message into the fewest digestible elements. Because people are by nature multifaceted, they often resist the whole process of limiting their defining quality. Most personal branders vacillate between two contradictory claims: even as they pay lip service to authenticity—the "old you"—they champion branding's revelatory results—the "brand-new you." Some are able to help clients bridge the gap, but the vast majority of branding specialists do not. At best, they simplify and spotlight, helping clients gain perspective and get organized. At worst, overzealous branders can be a waste of time and money as they confuse and disillusion their customers with questionable techniques and complex formulas for success.

Collectively, the personal branding movement is "supporting and developing an atmosphere" of formulaic, disposable identity, imposing a limiting vision on the most precious element of the human condition, the soul. There's simply no room for soul in an industry built on image and ego.

The Future of an
Illusion

top and look around. How many brands do you see? Ten? One hundred? The most obvious branded goods are often emblazoned with logos and labels and are fairly easy to identify: a cellular phone, a can of soda, a leather jacket. Naturally, the book you're holding is a brand. But don't stop there; so are its author, its publisher, and the retailers selling it. Even the particular font used to print the words you're reading and the photographer who took the author's photo on the jacket are brands in their own right. The world around us is composed of a dense patchwork of brands.

Today's branders understand a product's success by its ability to fulfill its so-called brand promise. But that notion is no longer limited to the realm of branding gurus; as consumers, we have similarly begun to expect a brand of everything. It's not difficult to understand why. Brands offer us mental shortcuts, helping us cut through the clutter of everything we buy and enabling us to communicate certain concepts quickly and easily. No one wants to sift through tens of thousands of packaged foods on every trip to the supermarket. Instead, we rely on the brands we know. And branding, when it's consistent, provides us with clarity and simplicity in a progressively hectic world. But branding has come unhinged from its initial principles, and its aims have become increasingly exaggerated and warped.

Although the branding movement grew out of our desire for consistency, consistency and reliability are among the casualties of the current obsessive branding disorder. Obsessive branding is what drives established quality brands to cut corners and sell cheaper products at Wal-Mart. The brand names still resonate with consumers, but the products are no longer the same. The same disorder is behind Procter & Gamble's campaigns to manipulate how we share information via word-of-mouth marketing. With an expanding army of hundreds of thousands of potentially covert marketers among us, we inevitably grow wary that things are not what they seem. And largely, they are not.

In the quest to strengthen consumer loyalty, branders have annexed our experiences and communities. Brand churches draw us into immersive environments where everything we encounter is managed. Brand tribes form around our favorite products, subsuming more traditional

forms of community with inherently shallow, fleeting co-
teries of consumer culture. Apple groupies fill chat rooms.
NASCAR adherents form minor cities at center track,
grilling branded meat and reading branded romance novels. Evangelists for hire, WOM marketers are awarded a
sense of belonging and connection in return for prosely-
tizing the latest bleach formula or pop album.

Branding is corrupting our culture by heralding emotion over reason, surface over core substance, and packaging over experience.

The problem isn't that we've adopted a philosophy in
which everything has a promise to fulfill. The problem
begins when we ask: A promise to whom? And from
whom? What, if anything, is the promise of the New Orleans "brand"? The answer varies for each tourist and
local business owner, each police officer, each social activist, and each victim of the city's escalating crime rate.
What, if anything, is your brand's promise? Of course,
there is no *one* answer. Each of us makes a range of vari-
able promises to the people in our lives. In turn, these
people have expectations of us. Branding acts to formalize
the world into brands, but to whom, if anyone, are all
these brands accountable? Surely no one. Yet the obsession spreads and the world slips further out of order.

When I began writing this book, I was thoroughly
amused by the extreme examples of branding that I saw.
Ads lasered into eggs? Straws and cornflakes engineered
to generate branded sounds? I rolled my eyes at branders'

starry-eyed proclamations that they would support and develop the atmosphere of anything they could get their hands on. Reinforcing my amusement was the belief that no matter how much we're inundated by marketing, people are simply too clever to let it get under their skin. I certainly thought I was.

Brands and branding exist in every sphere of my life. Branding permeates not just the clothes I wear and the food I eat, but my career. Everything about the book you're holding is subject to branding. My colleagues were quick to inform me that, as a writer, I had a brand to maintain and that I ought to market myself by setting up a website and a blog, by traveling the speaking circuit, and by networking with everyone I have ever worked with. Otherwise, how could I support and develop the atmosphere of *Obsessive Branding Disorder*? Other authors use promotional chotskies and events to help brand themselves; how about an *Obsessive Branding Disorder* pen, or the inaugural Obsessive Branding Awards? Perhaps I could build up a community by setting up an Obsessive Branding forum online or enlisting readers to join an OBD club, where they could enlighten others by sharing examples of branding in their lives (and spread the buzz about the book). Could the hypocrisy run any deeper?

But it was by examining the branding in my own life that I began to understand why branding has devolved into a disorder that corrodes the nature of identity. As brands encourage us to abandon reason, we tacitly adopt their lessons in our lives. Branding of one ilk or another encroaches upon our lives at every level, supplanting cultural bonds with the philosophy of reduction and deception. The social and individual risks are great. Every functioning society is in some way dependent on love, friendship, understanding, and trust. Conveniently, these are the aims of human relationships that, to a degree, have been self-sustaining throughout human history. Our obsession with branding has led us into a state of disorder in which society's fundamental relationships and institutions are being rapidly exploited by the aims of marketing.

The world is cheapened when everyone sees it with a marketer's eye. We lose trust for each other and grow skeptical of one another as we try to determine what we're being sold. We become more isolated and more self-conscious, more prone to rely on brands for status and to ally ourselves with other brand loyalists for company. All the while, we expect an enormous amount from brands and yet are disappointed at how poorly they meet our expectations.

Roused into awareness by the recent surge of branding in our society, we must look ourselves in the mirror and address our disorder head on. As obnoxious and intrusive as branding has become, we cannot allow ourselves the comfort of indifference. Indifference, after all, is the intent of "loyalty beyond reason"—a cleverly worded corporate battle cry for shortcutting critical thinking with emotion and lulling consumers into passivity. When we recognize that brands are courting our impulsive emotions, we can pause and consider the role of logic in the equation. And when we hear the siren call of personal branding, we can rely on authenticity rather than artificiality—for instance, when interviewing for a new job.

When we act collectively, our voices and purchasing decisions have the power to realign our culture. United, we can reclaim the control and community being co-opted by brands. As citizens, we stand to win back our public spaces, which are filled with more and more wasteful advertising clutter. As employees and business owners, we stand to win back the core principles that will ensure the future viability of our global markets. As individuals, we stand to win back a future in which corporate interests don't progressively encroach upon our private lives.

Without action, the excesses of branding will become more commonplace and accepted. As long as their citizens seem to be indifferent, city councils will continue to embrace the branding of communities, downplaying civic blemishes and simplifying their diverse character under a memorable motto or banner. Emboldened by consumer apathy, executives will grow accustomed to applying their innovations to marketing rather than to products and services. With no lack of volunteers, companies will continue sending out armies of clandestine propagandists to persuade their neighbors to buy goods in return for rewards, recognition, and more goods. Sensory branding will unleash a flood of branded scents, sounds, and colors throughout one industry after another, managing with corporate diligence the dynamic sensory environments in which we work, live, and play. Promising more invasive branding, advances in technology will afford companies more access to our private selves, decoding our facial expressions and deciphering our brain waves in the name of a more effective sales pitch. Saturated in branding, Americans will increasingly see themselves as brands—as goods defined more by their packaging than their contents.

To combat this obsessive branding disorder, we must acknowledge that we will always have brands—they are an inevitable medium for communication and commerce. Societies that have misjudged the value of symbols and icons have inevitably corrected themselves. In Soviet Russia goods were often labeled with no more than a description and a numerical code, but brands nevertheless persisted and wily citizens succeeded in identifying brands by matching factory codes to particular products. When certain factories were associated with tastier food and superior materials, their products inevitably achieved a certain identifiable "brand" status. In turn, societies that become overly obsessed with their icons eventually reject them.

Modern examples of brand removal have resulted in similar outcomes. *Adbusters*, the not-for-profit anticonsumerist magazine created in 1990 to "topple existing power structures and forge a major shift in the way we will live in the 21st century," has 120,000 subscribers in 60 countries around the world. Naomi Klein's polemical antiglobalization book, *No Logo*, has sold an estimated one million copies in some 27 languages. Yet, as Klein and *Adbusters* struggle to remove brands from our lives, even they cannot avoid branding. *Adbusters* sells its own brand of sneakers, calendars, flags, videos, "media empowerment kits," and a "culture jam book" (advertised as an "essential treatise" on what consumers can do to counteract America's "suicidal consumer binge"). *No Logo* has become, in Klein's reluctant admission, "a brand . . . in spite of itself." Subverting the dominant paradigm demands a strong brand apparently. Recognizing that brands have a place in society, it is up to us to determine where the balance is lost and the disorder begins.

We'll never be able to see through every branding illusion, of course. There will always be another fake website or documentary, always another overzealous neighbor with an ulterior motive. In fact, it will only get harder, because the very survival of brands relies on our failure to distinguish the reality from the brand. But if we acknowledge that we must rely on brands to some degree, and if we keep our focus on the products rather than the promotions, we can begin to extricate ourselves from a world of brand churches, tribes, and religion.

The effort to establish perspective and to distance ourselves from branding's influences is not without precedent. In 1927, in *The Future of an Illusion*, Sigmund Freud proposed that religion is the fruit of illusion—a set of comforting stories created to allay fears and uncertainty in an otherwise overwhelming world full of inexplicable realities. Though Freud wasn't particularly religious himself, he didn't object to the idea of illusions playing a profound role in people's lives. In fact, he argued that religion serves an important place in society by assuaging the individual's sense of helplessness in the world, uniting communities around a vision of a just and benevolent God, and helping to maintain social order by promising rewards for good behavior and punishment for bad behavior, both immediately and in the afterlife.

Beyond its utility, religion holds a place in culture, according to Freud, because it represents the innermost wishes of the individual. Illusions are not inherently false; they are more akin to wishful thinking. "For instance, a middle-class girl may have the illusion that a prince will come and marry her," writes Freud. "This is possible; and a few such cases have occurred. That the Messiah will come is much less likely. Whether one classifies this belief as illusion or something analogous to delusion will depend on one's personal attitude."[1]

Freud relied purely on science and logic and allowed little room for faith or mysticism in his analysis. But he also understood that most people prefer to believe in religion, and he had no illusions of starting a revolution. Ultimately, his goal was to convince others to apply intellect and reason in order to see their illusions for what they were. Such recognition could eventually afford people greater insight into themselves and into the human condition. If they chose to continue embracing their illusions, so be it.

Freud would have appreciated the parallels between religion and branding. In the grip of obsessive branding disorder, companies speak of their brands as if they are real things rather than wishes. Executives seek to formalize them, collecting brand laws in large company tombs, building temples to their brands, and baptizing customers in a sensory overload of branded smells and sounds. In turn, employees and consumers in the branded community fall into step, steeped in a branded experience that effectively bottles an ends as a means. Experiences and communities should spring forth organically, however, not roll off a production line. The brand is the ghost in the machine—a result of all the ingredients, not an ingredient itself. In reversing the natural order, we lionize an illusion.

Now stop and look around. How many illusions do you see?

NOTES

INTRODUCTION

1. Saison Research Institute survey, cited in Praso and Brady (2003).

2. Mike Embley, "You and Yours," BBC Radio 4, "Consumerism Japan," May 15, 2006; Louis-Vuitton website, comparison of Japan and France prices on various products, February 2008; Dana Thomas, *Deluxe: How Luxury Lost Its Luster* (New York: Penguin, 2007), p. 74.

3. Scott Robinette and Claire Brand, *The Hallmark Way of Winning Customers for Life* (New York: McGraw-Hill Professional, 2000), p. 29.

4. Kevin Roberts, *Lovemarks: The Future Beyond Brands* (Brooklyn, NY: powerHouse Books, 2004).

5. Robert Coen, "Insider's Report," Universal McCann, December 2007.

6. Chuck Lucier, Steven Wheeler, and Rolf Habbel, "The Era of the Inclusive Leader," *Strategy and Business* 47 (Summer 2007).

7. CMO Tenure Survey, Spencer Stuart, Inc. June 1, 2007.

8. Ron Hira and Philip E. Ross, "The R&D 100," *IEEE Spectrum*, (December 2007).

9. Workplace 2000 Employee Insight Survey.

10. Whittle Communications study, cited in Alison Leigh Cohen, "Advertising, Ad Clutter: Even in Restrooms Now," *New York Times*, February 18, 1988.

11. David W. Norton, Vice President, Experience Strategy and Research, Yamamoto Moss, "Toward Meaningful Brand Experiences," *Design Management Journal* (Winter 2003).

CHAPTER 1

1. "New Orleans Once Again Is U.S. Murder Capital," CNN.com, January 2, 2008.

2. Client lists from Cincinnati's leading branding firms. Crossed-checked with 2007 Fortune 100.

3. James Surowiecki, "The Decline of Brands," *Wired* (November 2004).

4. Dionne Searcy, "AT&T to 'Reintroduce' Itself with a Big Campaign," *Wall Street Journal*, December 29, 2005.

5. "Facts about P&G, 2007," http://www.pg.com.

6. Natalie Watson, "Profile: Cincinnati Riot Anniversary," NPR Weekend Edition, April 7, 2002.

7. Dan Horn, "The Riots Explode: A City's Dark Week," *Cincinnati Enquirer*, December 30, 2001.

8. "100 Leading National Advertisers," *Advertising Age*, June 2007.

9. Barry M. Horstman, "Boycott Has Tested the City's Resilience," *Cincinnati Post,* April 17, 2002.

10. Nathaniel Popper, "Israel Aims to Improve Its Public Image," *Jewish Daily Forward*, October 14, 2005.

11. Gary Rosenblatt, "Marketing a New Image," *Jewish Week*, January 20, 2005.

12. Chris Moon, "The Selling of Kansas," *Topeka Capital-Journal,* January 8, 2005; Brand Oregon, Advisory Board Minutes Meeting, August 5, 2004; "NE Tourism Campaign Glance," AP Newswires, June 15, 2006.

13. Gene Johnson, "Seattle's 'Say WA' Says Goodbye; City Adopts New Slogan" (AP), *Seattle Times*, October 21, 2006.

14. Dan Fitzpatrick, "Pittsburgh Commmittee Generates 'Brand Messages' for Region," Knight Ridder/Tribune Business News, April 15, 2003.

15. Vincent M. Mallozzi, "Jersey: How About If You've Got the Time, We've Got the State," *New York Times,* May 28, 2006.

16. Joe Stinebaker, "Galveston Looking to Polish Image," Associated Press, December 18, 2006.

17. Tom Loftus, "Audit: State May Have Overpaid 'Unbridled Spirit' Firm," *Louisville Courier-Journal,* November 1, 2006.

18. Connecticut Commission on Culture and Tourism, "All Five Regions Sell Individual Identity to Support 'Connect' Campaign" (press release), May 23, 2005.

19. "City Crime Rankings," CQ Press/Morgan Quinto Press, 2007.

20. Kevin Osborne, "Streicher Says We're Safe," *City Beat*, September 13, 2006.

CHAPTER 2

1. "Will She, Won't She?" *The Economist*, August 9, 2007.

2. "How Targeted Collaboration Between Retailers and Manufacturers Promotes the Success of New Product Launches," National Association of Chain Drug Stores, with PricewaterhouseCoopers, March 22, 2007.

3. Gordon Fairclough, "From Hongda to WuMart; Brand Names in China Have Familiar, if Off-Key, Ring," *Wall Street Journal*, October 19, 2006.

4. Tim Phillips, *Knockoff: The Deadly Trade in Counterfeit Goods* (London: Kogan Page, 2005), pp. 35–37.

5. Keith Lincoln and Lars Thomassen, *Private Label* (London: Kogan Page, 2008).

6. Rob Walker, "Consumed: Ol' Roy," *New York Times,* February 22, 2004.

7. Edward Reilly and Jay Jamrog, "The Quest for Innovation: A Global Study in Innovation Management, 2006–2016," study commissioned by American Management Association, conducted by Human Research Institute, April 20, 2006.

8. *Key Indicators of the Labor Market*, 5th ed. (Geneva: International Labor Office, 2007).

9. Simon Bowers, "Unilever to Axe 20,000 Jobs," *Guardian,* August 2, 2007.

10. Donna Goodison, "Zara: Doing It By the Numbers," *Boston Herald*, October 14, 2007.

CHAPTER 3

1. Jack Trout, "Trout on Strategy," (New York: McGraw-Hill Professional, 2004), p. 3.

2. Scott Robinett and Claire Brand, *Emotional Marketing: The Hallmark Way of Winning Customers for Life* (New York: McGraw-Hill Professional, 2000), p. 29.

3. Claudia H. Deutsch, "Charmin to New York: 'Go in Style,'" *New York Times,* Novemeber 11, 2006.

4. Cotton Timberlake, "Popping the Question: Today's Brides Covet Square Diamond Rings," Bloomberg, November 26, 2007.

5. Barry Kaplan, "Forever Diamonds," www.jewelry-paideia.com.

6. Miller McPherson, Lynn Smith-Lovin, and Matthew E. Brashears, "Social Isolation in America: Changes in Core Discussion Networks over Two Decades," *American Sociological Review* (June 2006).

7. Jonathan Clements, "Money and Happiness: Will You Laugh All the Way to the Bank?" *Wall Street Journal*, August 17, 2006.

8. Martin Lindstrom, *BRAND Sense* (New York: Free Press, 2005), p. 5.

9. Philip Elmer-DeWitt, "Report: Apple Stores Outperform Best Buy, Saks, and Tiffany," *Fortune*, Apple 2.0 blog.

9. Laura Heller, "The New Nokia Store—the Best Place to Buy a $90,000 cell phone," DSN Retailing Today, July 10, 2006.

11. Jim Edwards, "Broken Promises" (BrandWeek/Brand Keys Customer Loyalty Index), *BrandWeek* (May 2006).

CHAPTER 4

1. Sara Kehavlani Goo, "Apple Gets a Big Slice of the Product Placement Pie," *Washington Post,* April 15, 2006.

2. Gail Schiller, "*Talladega Nights* in High Gear with Products," *The Hollywood Reporter*, August 3, 2006.

3. Eric Pfanner, "On Advertising: Just for Men—A Dirty Story," *International Herald Tribune*, July 16, 2006.

4. Jean Halliday, "Mercedes Launches Ad Blitz to Recoup Lost Ground," Adage.com, January 31, 2006.

5. J. Walter Smith, president, Yankelovich, speech given at American Association of Advertising Agencies, April 2004.

6. Annual advertising estimates from Robert J. Coen, Maccam Erickson, Inc., and *Advertising Age*.

7. Joe Mandese, "'Good News' Is Bad News for Magazines, Brand Makes Editorial Demand," *MediaDailyNews*, October 10, 2005.

8. Magz Osborne, "Do or Die," Television Asia, October 2003.

9. Pamela Parke, "Billion-Dollar Brands' Word-of-Mouth Ambitions," *The Click2 Network*, June 23, 2006.

10. Greg Ireland, "Worldwide and U.S. DVR 2004–2008 Forecast," International Data Corporation, March 14, 2004.

11. "Do Not Call Registrations Exceed 10 Million," (press release), FTC, June 2003.

12. "The State of Spam," Symantec, February 2008.

13. Laura Baverman, "Kroger Testing if Conveyer Belt Ads Give Grocer Pep in Its Profit," Business First of Columbus, November 8, 2006.

14. Alex Kingsbury and Lindsey Galloway, "Textbooks Enter the Digital Era," *U.S. News & World Report,* October 8, 2006.

15. Suzanne Vranica, "Ad Buyers Eye Clear Channel's 'Blink' Spots," *Wall Street Journal*, November 2, 2006.

16. Anju Mary Paul, "Pregnant Bellies Auctioned as Ad Space on eBay," *Women's Enews*, March 19, 2006.

17. "Children—A New Advertising Medium?" *Gush* magazine (n.d.).

18. Christopher Simmons, "Mother Gives Birth to Bouncing Baby Ad" (press release), *Send2Press Newswire*, May 28, 2005.

19. Aaron Falk, "Mom Sells Face Space for Tattoo Advertisement," *Desert Morning News*, June 30, 2005.

20. "Product Placement in the Pews? Microtargeting Meets Megachurches," *Knowledge@Wharton*, November 15, 2006.

CHAPTER 5

1. John Horn, "The Reviewer Who Wasn't There," *Newsweek Web*, June 2, 2001.

2. "Sony Pays $1.5 Milion Over Fake Critic," BBC News Online, August 3, 2005.

3. Emily Engelman, "The Mystery of Dalaro: Fact or Fiction?" Ford Communications Network (n.d.).

4. Chris Kohler, "Sony's Failed PSP Viral Marketing Stunt," *Wired Blog*, December 4, 2006.

5. Michael Barbaro, "Wal-Mart Enlists Bloggers in PR Campaign," *New York Times,* March 7, 2006.

6. Pallaui Gogoi, "Walmart's Jim and Laura: The Real Story," *Businessweek,* November 27, 2006.

7. "Word of Mouth Marketing Forcast, 2007–2011," PQ Media, November 2007.

8. Robert Berner, "I Sold It Through the Grapevine," *Businessweek*, May 19, 2006.

9. "Where's Debbie?" MEC MediaLab, April 2004.

10. Berner 2006; Matthew Cralmer, "Is Buzz Marketing Illegal?" *Advertising Age,* October 3, 2005.

11. Mary K. Engle, "Staff Opinion Letter," FTC, December 7, 2006.

12. James Heyman and Dan Ariely, "Effort for Payment: A Tale of Two Markets," *Psychological Science* (November 2004).

13. Walter J. Carl, "To Tell or Not to Tell," *Northwestern University Communication Studies* (January 2006).

CHAPTER 6

1. Jim Hinckley and Jon G. Robinson, *The Big Book of Car Culture: The Armchair Guide to Automotive America* (Motorbooks/MBI Publishing Company, 2005), pp. 50–51.

2. Martin Lindstrom, Brandsense research.

3. Rachael Gordon, "Ad Firm with a First—but Will it Whiff by Mixing Cookies, Muni?" *San Francisco Chronicle*, November 30, 2006.

4. Chris Paukert, "Gentlemen, Start Your Barbecues! NASCAR-Branded Meats Are Here," *Autoblog*, March 30, 2006.

5. www.nascar.com/guides/about/nassar.

6. Holly M. Sanders, "Court TV Has Creepy 'Whisper' Campaign," *New York Post,* November 8, 2006.

7. Gregory Solman, "Microsoft Preps Big Spend for Zone MP3 Player," *Adweek,* November 16, 2006.

CHAPTER 7

1. Ryan Underwood, "Jonesing for Soda," *Fast Company* (March 2005).

2. *Supermarket News.*

3. "Best Global Brands 2007," Interbrand.

4. Samuel M. McClure et al., "Neural Correlates of Behavioral Preface for Culturally Familiar Drinks," *Neuron* 44, no. 2 (October 14, 2004), pp. 379–387.

5. "100 Leading National Advertisers," *Advertising Age*, June 25, 2007.

6. Hoovers, Inc.

CHAPTER 8

1. Lloyd Grove and Hudson Morgan, "Stern 'Q&A' Raises Questions," *New York Daily News*, June 1, 2004.

2. Estimate by Charles Riotto president of Licensing Industry Merchandisers Association, cited in Angela Phipps Towle, "Celebrity Branding," *The Hollywood Reporter*, November 18, 2003.

3. WPP Group.

4. John LaRosa, "The U.S. Market for Self-Improvement Products and Services," Marketdata Enterprises, Inc., September 1, 2006.

CHAPTER 9

1. Sigmund Freud, *The Future of an Illusion* (1927; reprint, New York: W. W. Norton, 1961).

ACKNOWLEDGMENTS

This book began as an essay in the October 2005 issue of *Fast Company*. A number of people have helped make it a reality.

It was my editor, David Lidsky, who first shared my fascination with the branding world and encouraged me to explore it further. This book—and many of the opportunities in my career—would not have been possible without his unique friendship, insight, and humor.

Fast Company's manifesto declares first and foremost that work is personal. The founding editors who wrote and lived those words, William Taylor and Alan Webber, were the same editors who instilled in me their importance when they hired me as a fact checker in 2002. Their guidance and patience are qualities every employee desires from his or her work.

Few writers are fortunate enough to have an agent as brilliant as Stephen Hanselman by their side. Stephen's enthusiasm for the original essay inspired me to write the proposal, and I won the contract, in large part, because of his savvy and persistence. Cynicism is a long-standing tradition in publishing—one from which I am not entirely immune; working with Stephen, anything seems possible.

I owe much to the unflagging support of my publisher, Susan Weinberg, and my editors at PublicAffairs—David Patterson, Clive Priddle and Morgen VanVorst. Susan and David, who brought me on board; Clive, who carefully shepherded the book; and Morgen, who brought new life to the manuscript (and to my resolve) in the final march.

I want to thank the branders featured throughout the book for their candor and perspective, in particular Martin Lindstrom and Audrey Arbeeny. Often shrewd and self-aware, they provoked me to weigh the contradictions and consequences of their field with the type of empathy journalists must bring to their subjects.

I am deeply appreciative for the support and camaraderie of many others who have helped me personally and professionally, among them William Langewiesche, Cullen Murphy, Nate Nickerson, Charles Fishman, Keith Hammonds, John Byrne, Mark Vamos, Lynn Moloney, Danielle Sacks, Julia Serebrinsky, The Hostel, and Diza Sauers.

And finally, my gratitude to my parents, Christopher and Katharine, whose steadfast belief in me continues to cultivate my belief in myself.

INDEX

Lucas Conley, who began his career at *The Atlantic Monthly,* is a contributing writer for *Fast Company.* His work has appeared in *The Boston Globe* and *ESPN: The Magazine,* among other publications. *Obsessive Branding Disorder* is his first book. He lives in Santa Fe, New Mexico.